Contents

W9-CEO-332

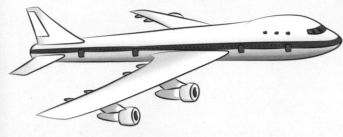

James Mravec is the author and illustrator of *You Can Draw Animals* and *You Can Draw Dinosaurs*. His illustrations have appeared in numerous books, science fiction magazines, and greeting cards. He is currently a freelance illustrator, as well as a teacher at the Cleveland Institute of Art, where he also received a Bachelor of Fine Arts in Illustration and Graphic Design.

Louis Weber, CEO
Publications International, Ltd.
7373 North Cicero Avenue
Lincolnwood, Illinois 60712

Permission is never granted for commercial purposes.

Manufactured in China.

8 7 6 5 4 3 2 1

ISBN: 1-4127-0564-9

Becoming an Artist

Getting Started

Drawing is not as hard as you may think. One of the secrets of drawing is that any object can be broken down into smaller parts. By following the step-by-step instructions in this book, you can use this secret to draw many kinds of boats, planes, and trains. By copying these pictures, you will learn basic drawing skills.

You'll need some basic tools: pencil, pencil sharpener, eraser, felt-tip pen, and grid paper. Make photocopies of the grid paper at the back of this book if you need more.

The illustrations start with large shapes. Draw the full shape, even if all of it will not be seen in the final drawing. You can erase the part you don't need. In each step you will add more detail. The steps are colored to show exactly what to draw when. The lines for each new step are red, while the lines from previous steps are gray.

Each drawing is shown on a grid. When you are making the step-by-step drawings, look closely at how the lines and shapes fit on the grid, and copy them onto your grid sheet.

After all the steps are drawn, use a felt-tip pen to go over the pencil lines. Ink only over the lines you need in the final drawing. Give the ink some time to dry so it won't smear, then erase the extra pencil lines. There's your completed drawing! Now you are ready to color the drawing.

Coloring Your Drawings

Start coloring with tools that are familiar to you. If you enjoy coloring with crayons, use them. When you get more comfortable with coloring, you can try other methods such as colored pencils, watercolor paints, markers, or even artist's chalk.

Pick colors that fit the drawing. But be creative! Lightly add the main color to the drawing. Some of the vehicles may already have designs on them, so you can use several different colors. Keep the colors light in the beginning—it is easier to make a color darker than to make it lighter. After the main color is finished, gently add darker colors to areas that would be in shadows. This is called shading and helps the drawing look more realistic.

After shading, add lighter colors where more light would be. This is called highlighting, and it is usually done on the top areas of the shapes. Think of the sun lighting the vehicle from above. Look at the color pictures in the book, and try to copy the light and dark shading of the colors. Once you fill in all the colors, your illustration is complete!

Pirate Ship

Be sure to use the center of the graph paper so you don't run off the page with your drawing.

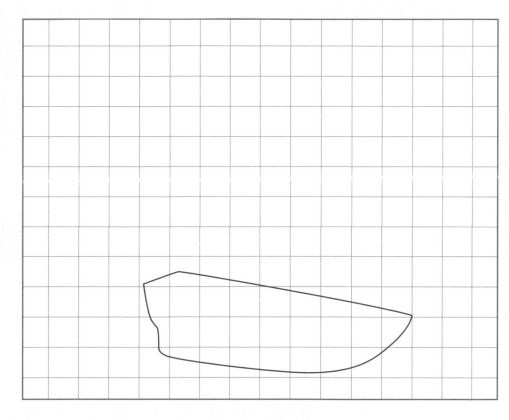

1. Draw the long, triangular main form for the boat.

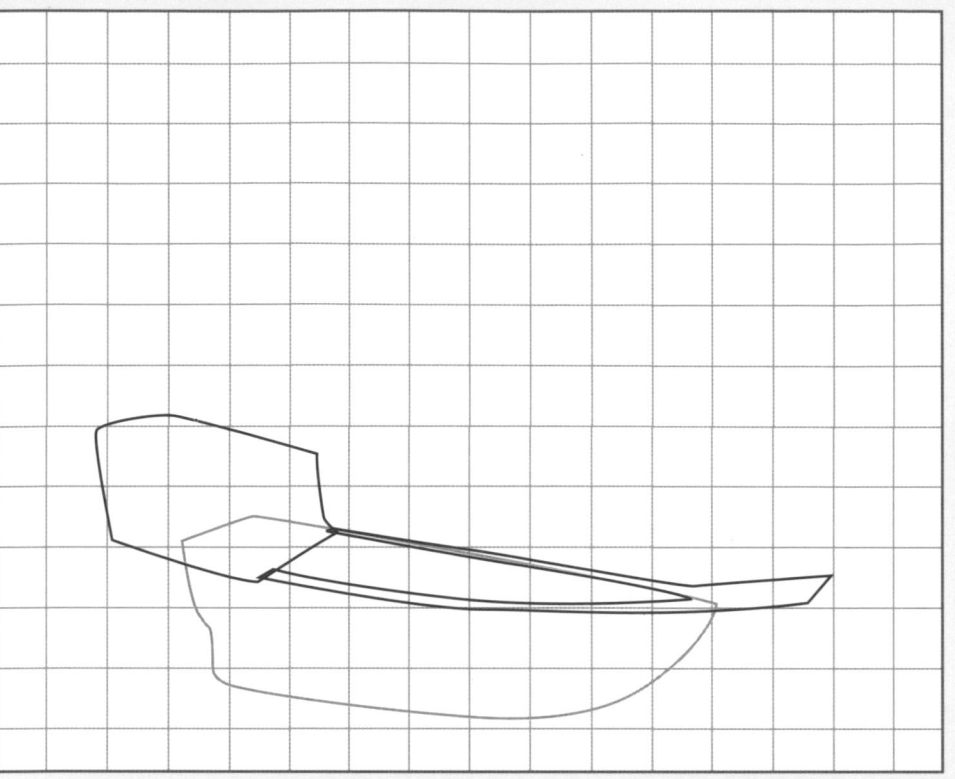

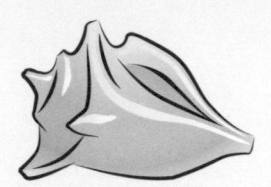

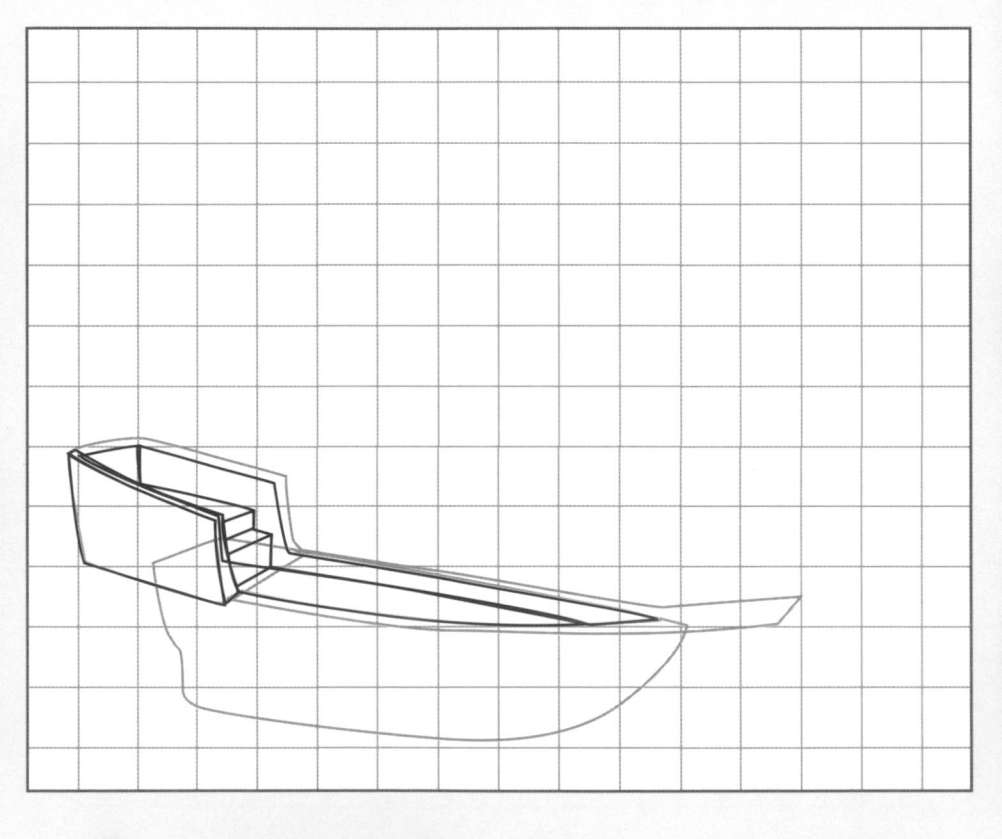

2. Add an angled shape on the back end of the boat. Draw a line along the side of the boat, and continue it on to form a post coming off the front end of the ship. Bring the line back along the far side of the hull.

3. Outline the back shape and the top of the boat's hull to add depth and create the ship's deck. Use stacked rectangles to add details to the back deck and deck steps.

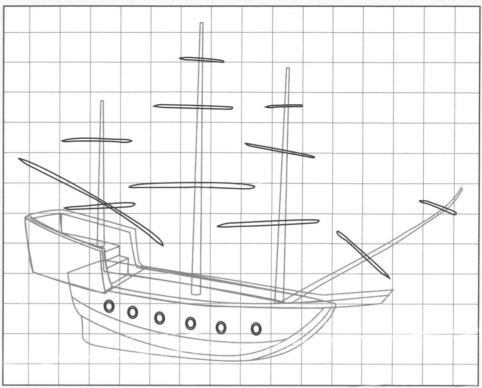

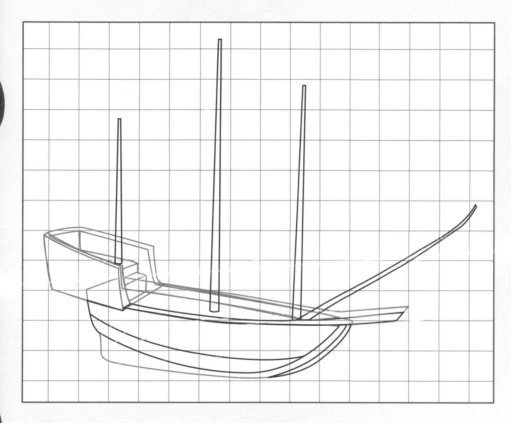

5. Sketch long, thin sticks on the masts to create the crossbars. Add six circular porthole windows on the boat's side.

4. Draw three tall masts rising from the deck. Add a fourth mast angling forward from the deck. Draw a long, curved bar that extends to the end of the post on the boat's tip. Use lines to sketch some side beam details on the hull.

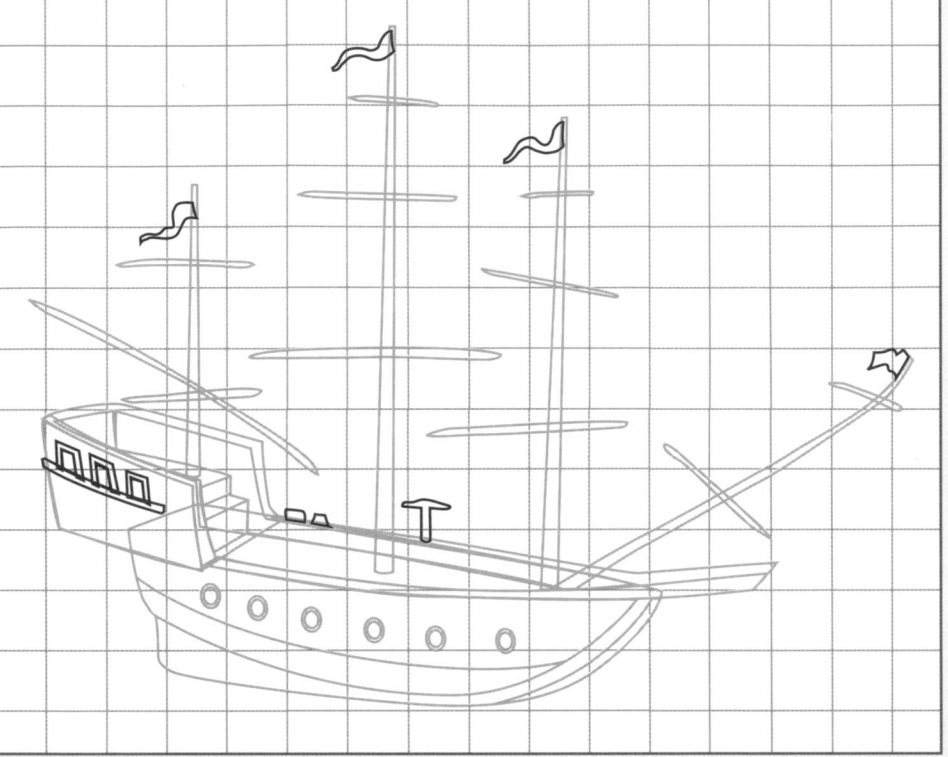

6. Draw three rectangular windows on the back of the ship. Add a long, thin rectangle underneath them to create detail. Sketch flags on each mast. Draw two small wedges and a shape like a pickax on the far side of the deck.

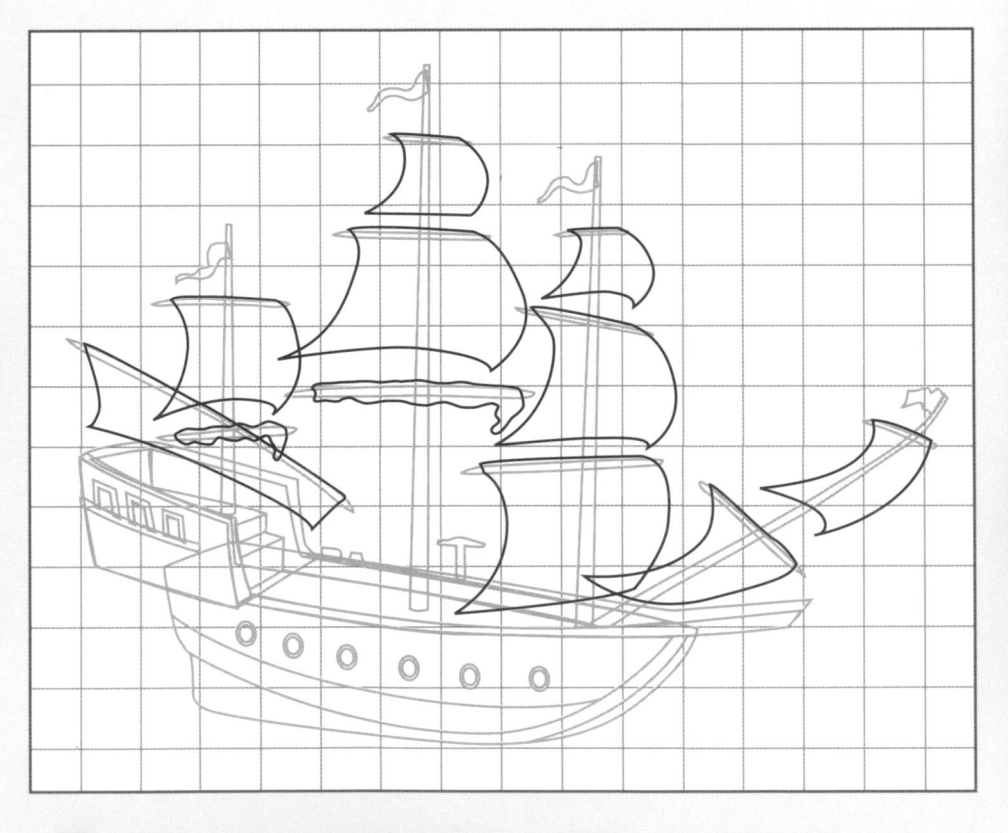

7. Draw sails using the crossbars and masts as guides. The lowest sails on the back two masts are rolled up on the crossbars. To create this look, draw a squiggly-lined rectangular shape.

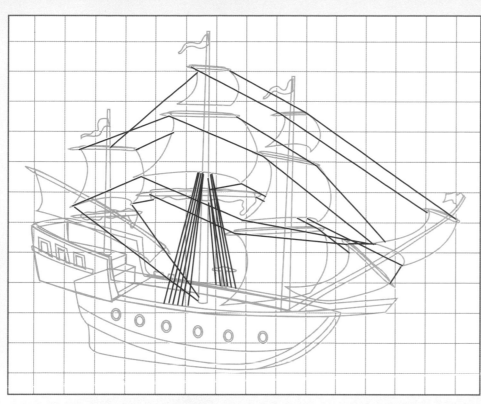

8. Draw lines going from one crossbar to another. Add several lines angling down from the center mast.

9. Trace the pencil lines you want to keep with a felt-tip pen. Erase any extra lines.

Sailboat

1. Start the sailboat with two big curved triangles for the sails. Add a pointed shape for the hull.

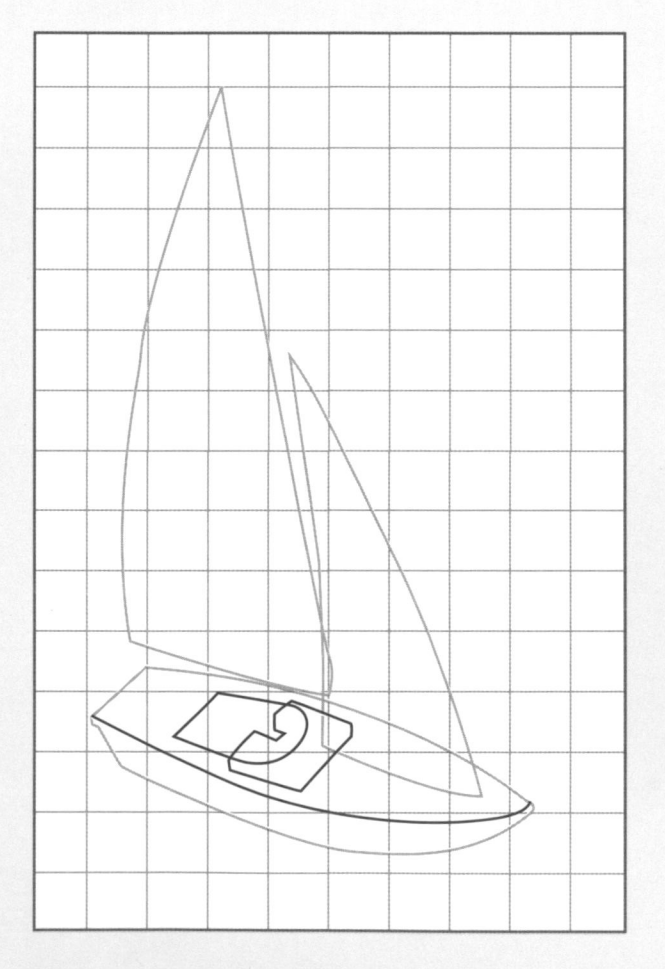

2. Draw a curved line to form the side of the hull. Sketch a rectangle with a rounded end for the seating area. Add a fat bracket shape on top of it.

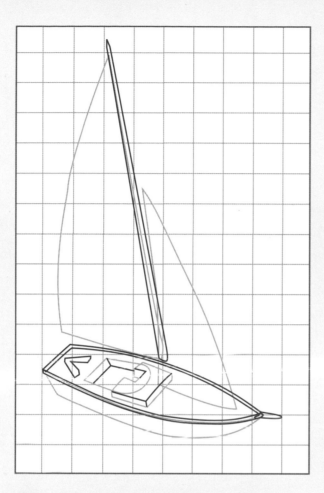

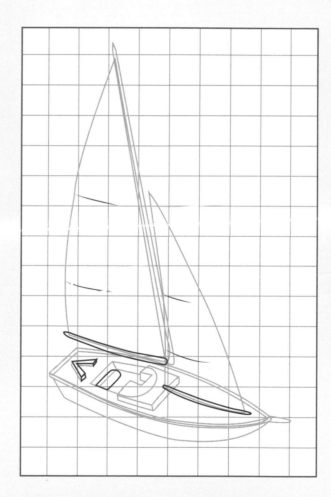

3. Draw the mast between the sails. Add edge lines following the hull. Sketch a V-shape bar to create deck detail, and add lines for depth in the seating area. Draw a small post on the front of the boat.

4. Add rectangular crossbars at the bottom of both sails. Draw detail lines on the V shape and in the seating space. Add detail lines to each sail.

5. Draw wavy lines under the boat for the water.

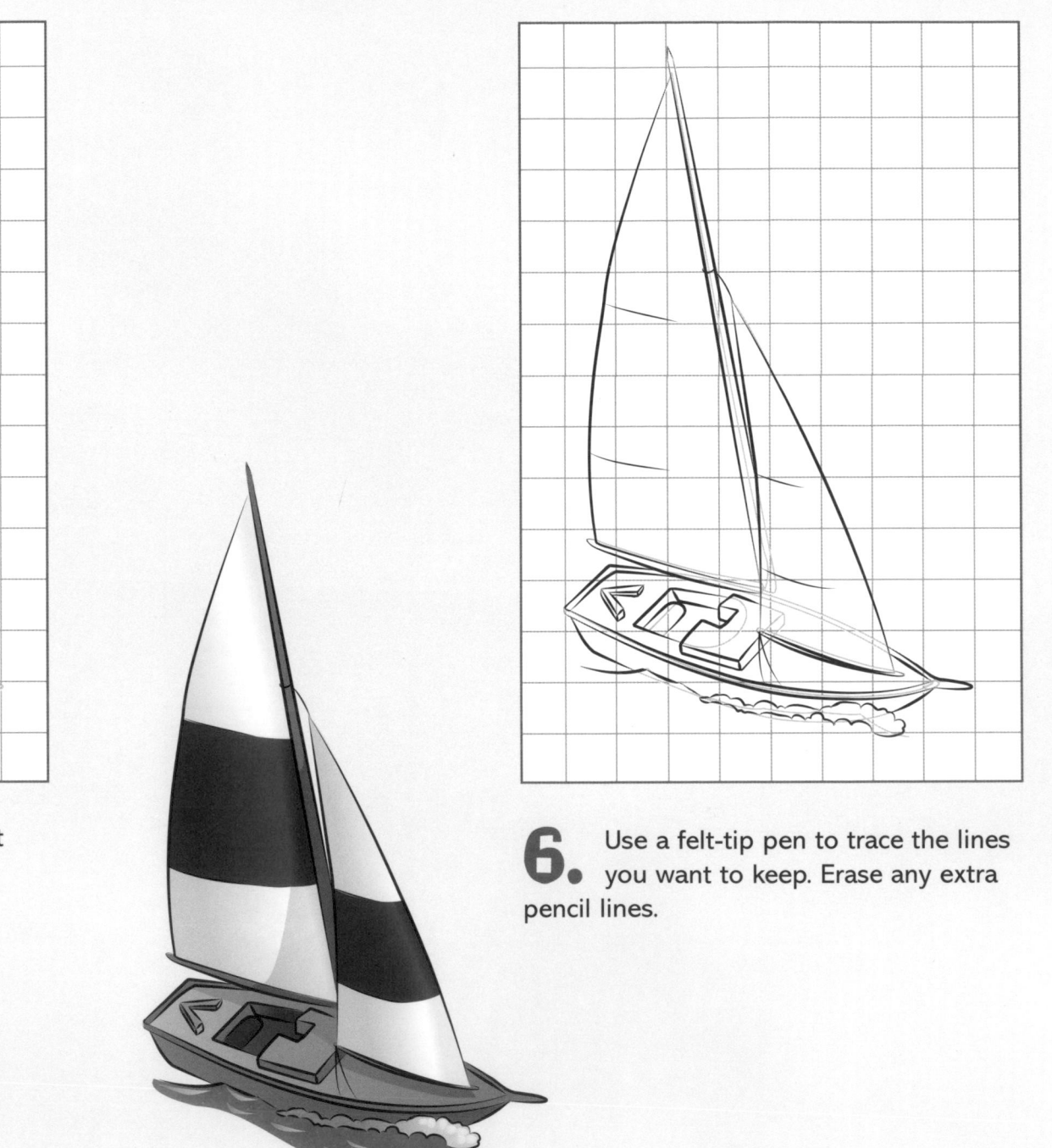

6. Use a felt-tip pen to trace the lines you want to keep. Erase any extra pencil lines.

Submarine

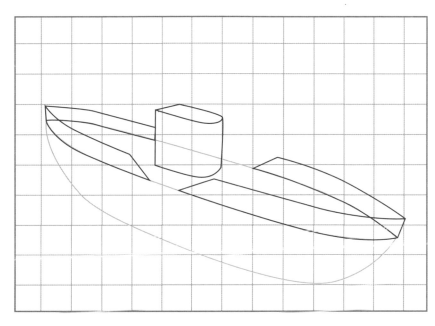

2. Draw a rectangular shape with two curved edges in the center of the deck. Add a curved line toward the top of the shape to create a U-shape block. Sketch four rectangular shapes to create the rails on the edge of the deck.

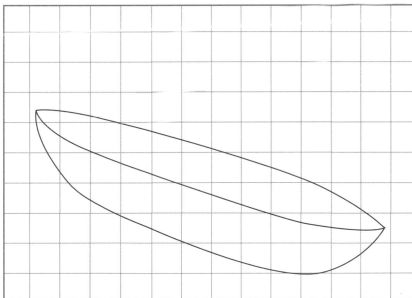

1. Draw a long football-like shape for the main body of the submarine. Add a curved line from one point to the other to create the side of the boat.

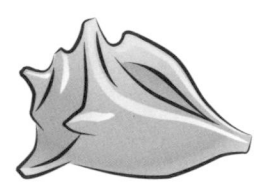

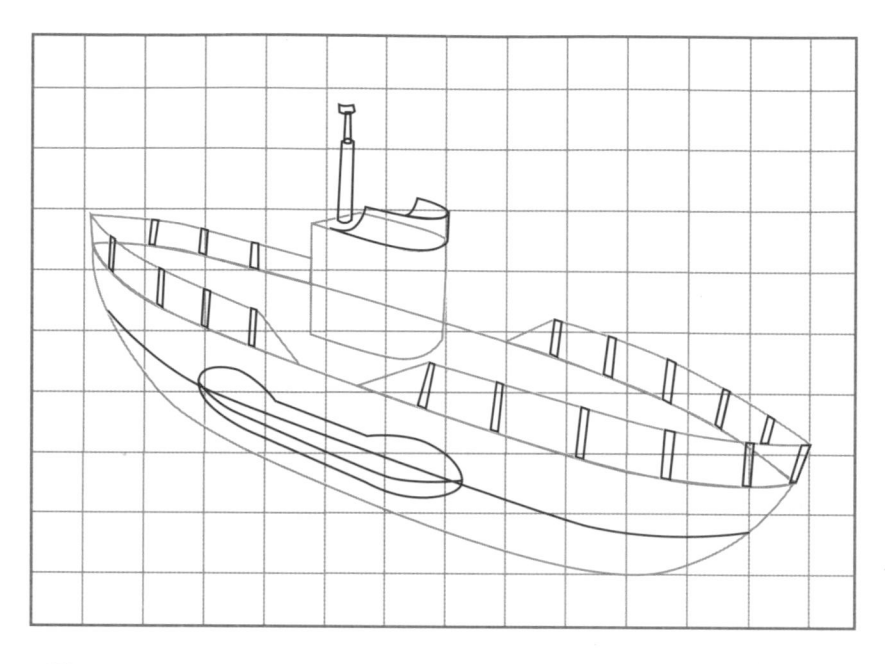

3. Draw a railing on top of the U-shape block. Add thin cylinders to make the periscope tower on top. Sketch some short bars on the side railings. Draw a curved line along the side of the sub. Add an oblong oval shape on the side, and divide it with a curved line.

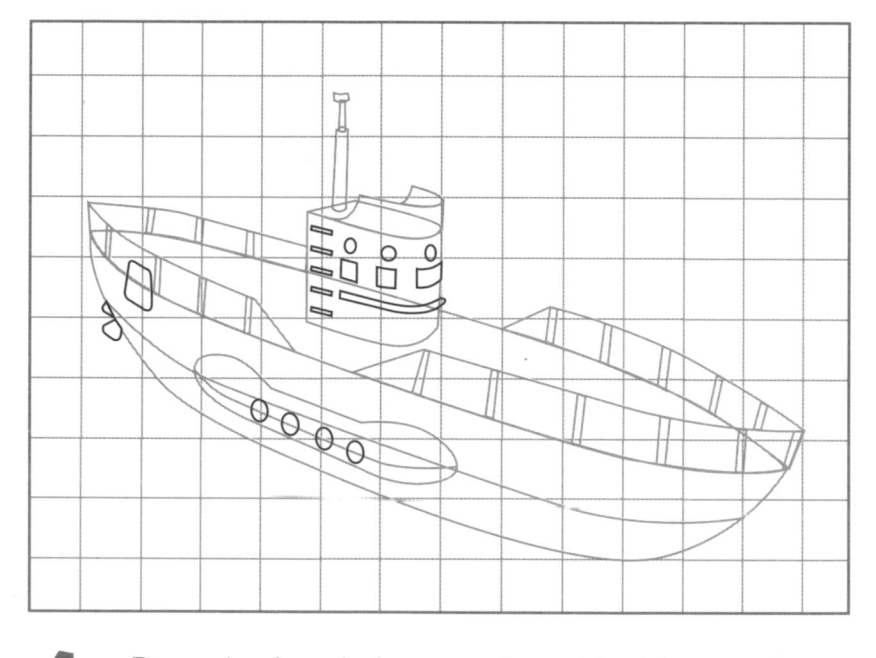

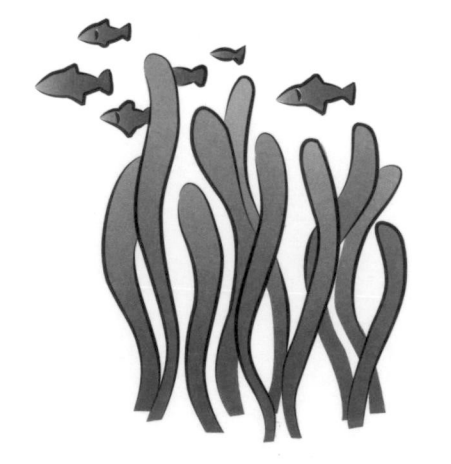

4. Draw circular windows on the sub's side as well as near the top of the U-shape block. Also, add rectangular windows to the block and some thin rectangles for details. Sketch the wedge shapes of the propeller at the back of the sub. Add a hatch rectangle toward the back end of the sub.

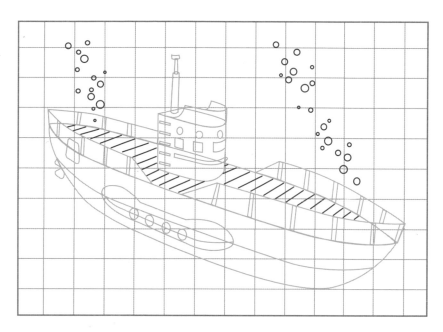

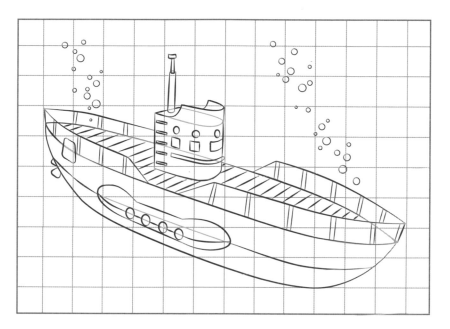

5. Sketch lines cutting across the deck. Add bubbles floating up from the sub.

6. Use a felt-tip pen to trace the lines you want to keep. Erase any extra pencil lines.

Navy Ship

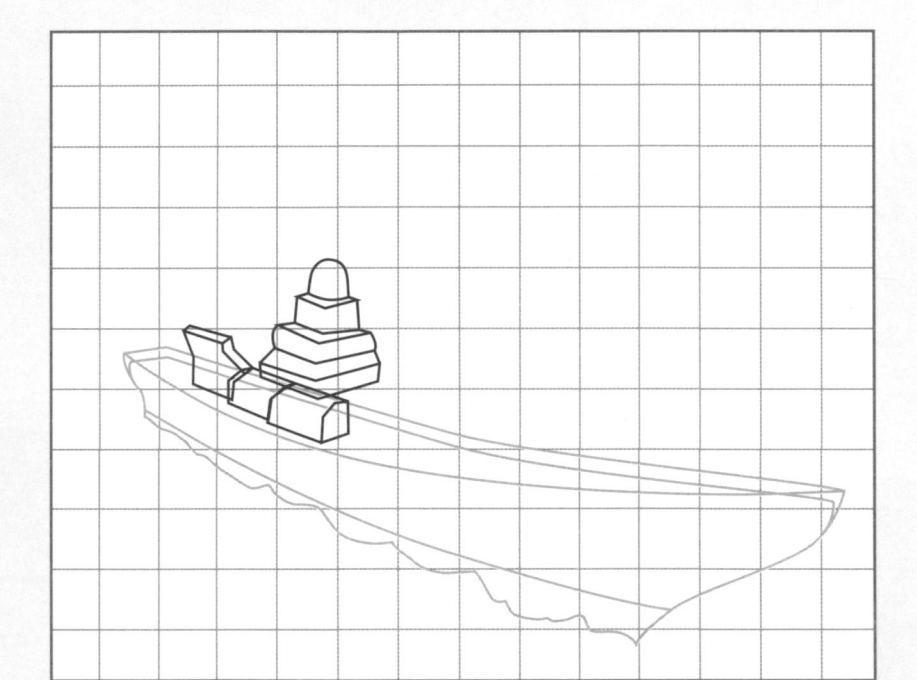

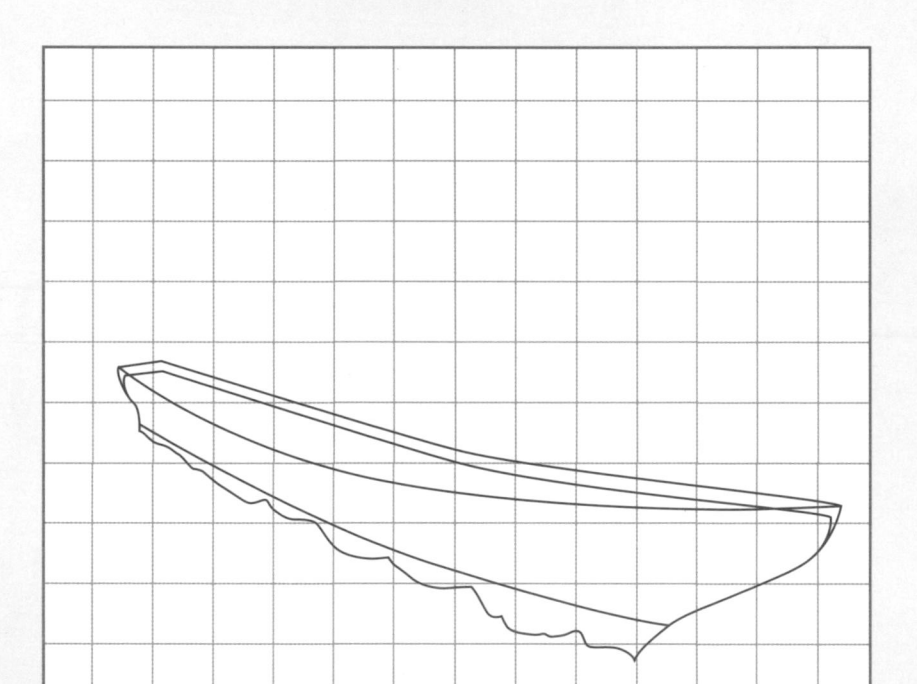

1. Start with a long banana shape to make the hull of the ship. Outline the lines of the hull to add depth and create the deck. Sketch a wavy line across the side of the boat to create the water level.

2. Draw stacked geometric shapes toward the back of the boat. Draw a half-oval at the top of the stack. This forms part of the ship's upper structure. (This can be difficult, but just follow the lines shown.) Add a shape jutting up at the back of the deck. Draw lines in it to create dimension.

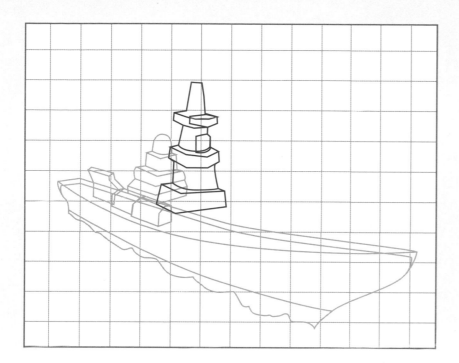

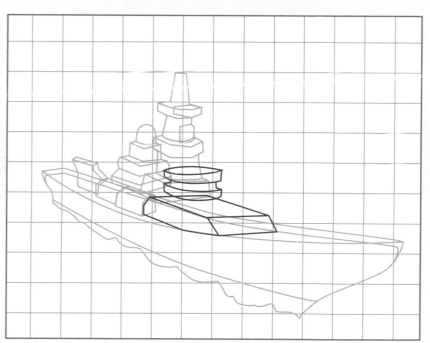

3. Just in front of your first structure, draw some cubes and cylinders on top of each other. (Again, just follow the lines as you see them.) This creates the ship's center structure.

4. Add a long, flat box toward the front of the boat. Sketch a couple of short, fat cylinders on top of it.

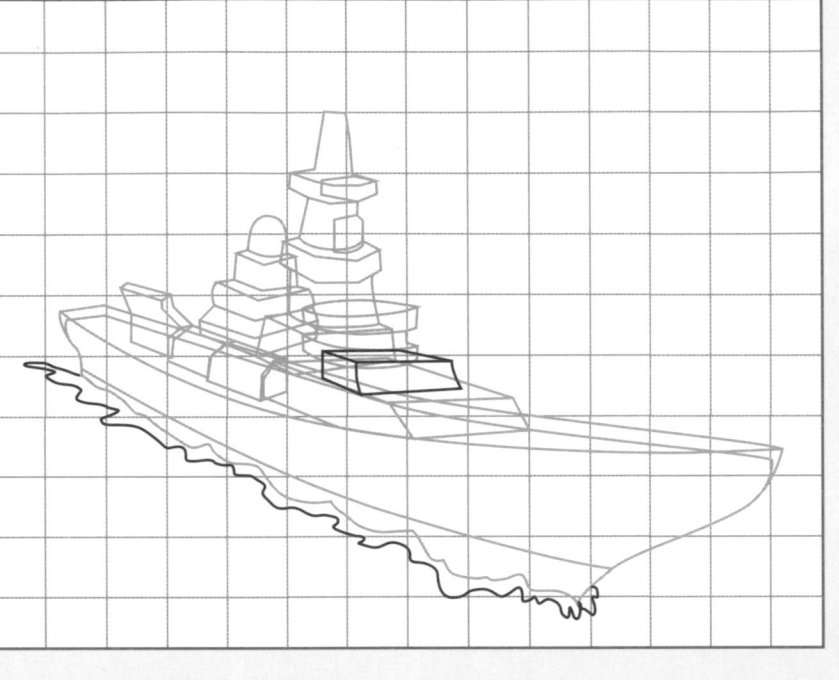

5. Draw a smaller box on top of the first flat box. Sketch in some wavy lines to form the waves under the ship.

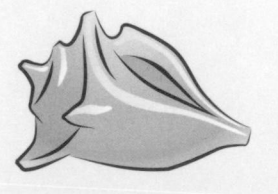

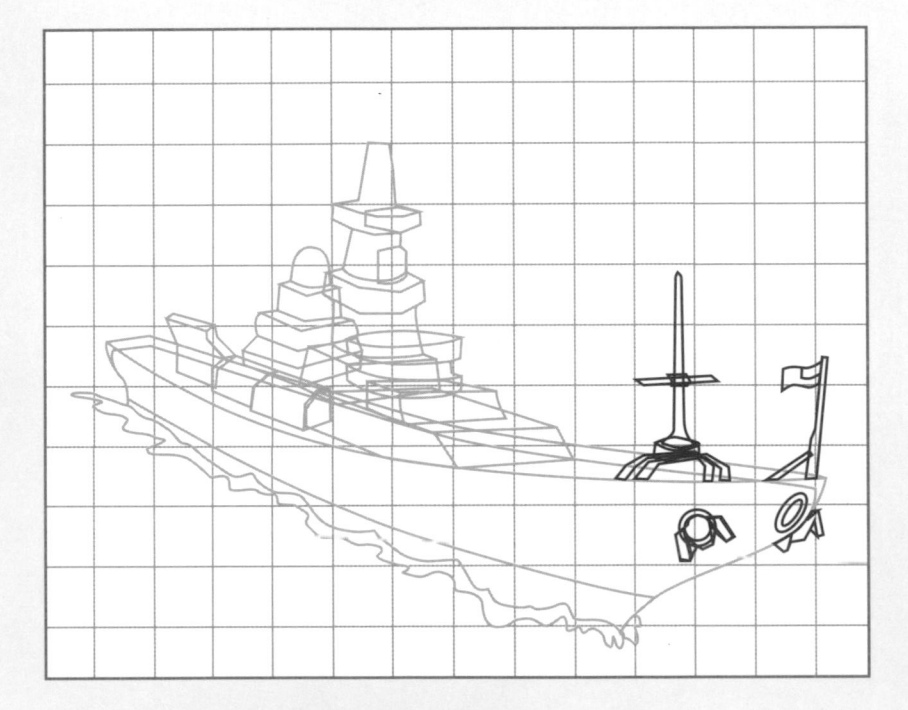

6. Sketch an antenna at the front of the ship. Add a flagpole next to it. Draw two circles within circles on the boat's side for windows. Draw small rectangles next to the nearest window to create the anchor detail. Add small rectangles and a wedge shape to the far side of the boat's front to create an anchor detail.

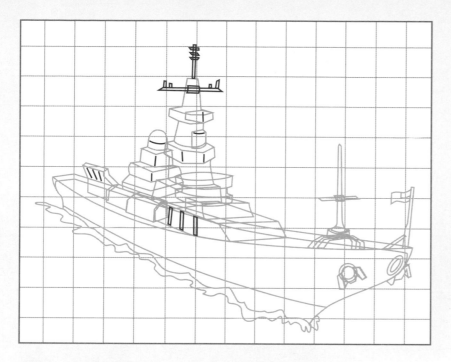

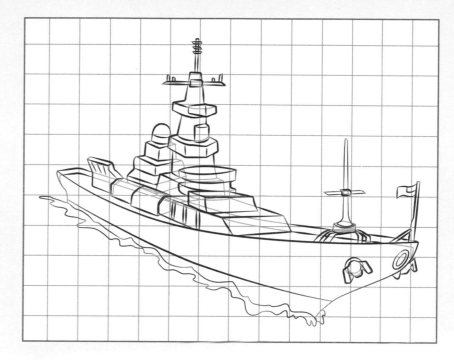

7. Finish with some detail lines on the upper structures. Add a crossbar and antenna to the tallest structure.

8. Trace the pencil lines you want to keep with a felt-tip pen. Erase any extra lines.

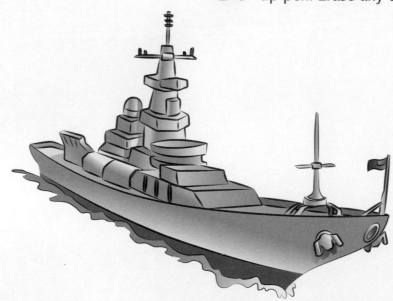

Biplane

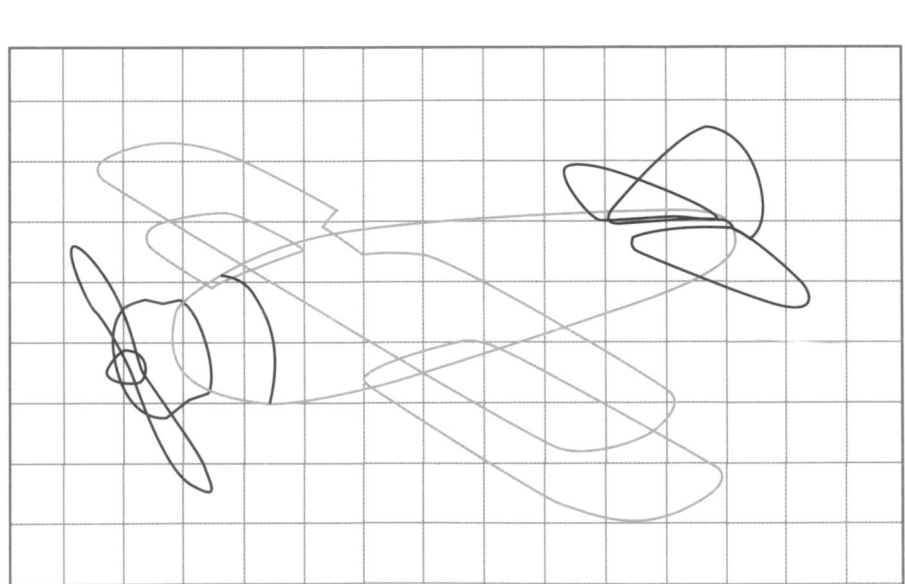

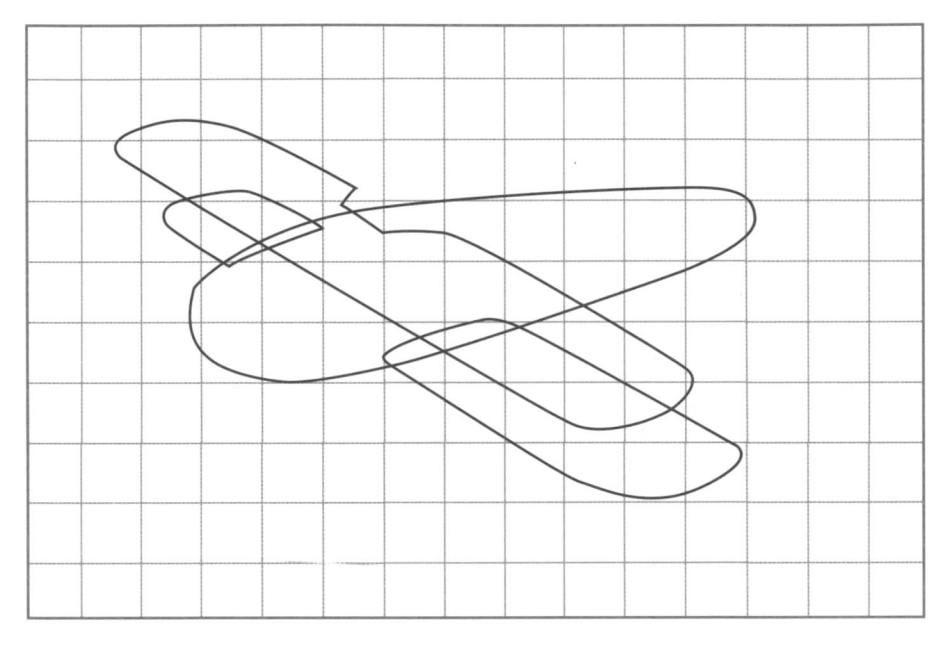

1. Start drawing the plane with a long oval for the main body. Put a short, rounded-off rectangle on both sides of the body to create the lower wings. Add a longer, rounded-off rectangle with a notch in the middle to form the top wings.

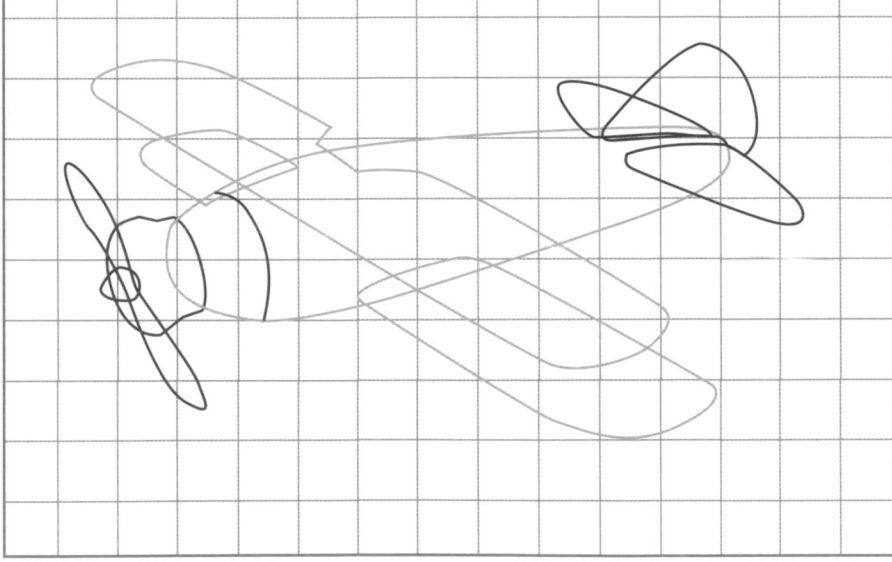

2. Sketch three rounded triangles for the tail. Draw a curved line near the tip of the plane to form the nose. Sketch a doorknob shape at the plane's tip. Add a cone and two long, thin ovals to form the propeller.

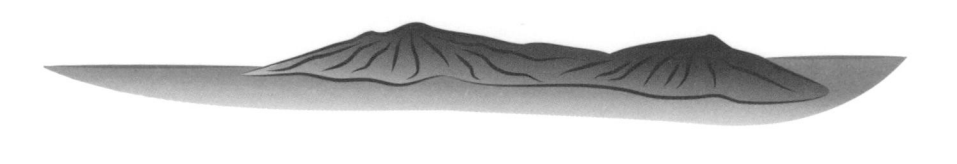

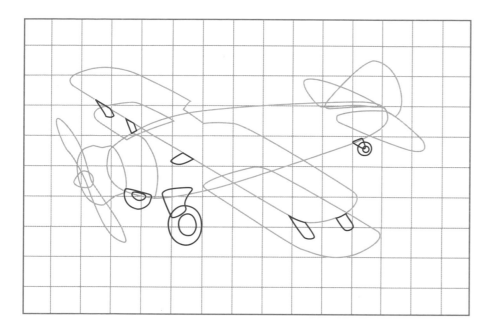

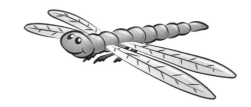

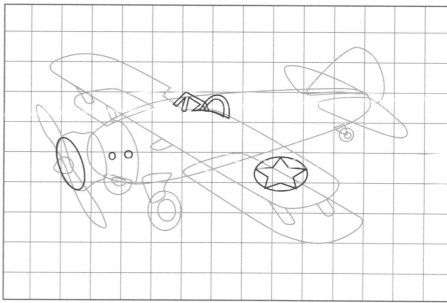

3. Sketch a wedge shape at the front and back of the plane to create the wheel supports. Draw three wheels—one small one under the tail and two larger ones under the wings. Add rectangular support beams from the bottom wings to the top wings and two from the body to the top wings.

To complete each drawing correctly, be sure to go through the steps in order.

4. Sketch the lines for the windshield at the indented part of the top wing. Just behind that, draw two half-ovals to create the seat. Sketch an oval and some small circles to add detail to the nose. Draw a star inside of a circle on the tip of the top wing.

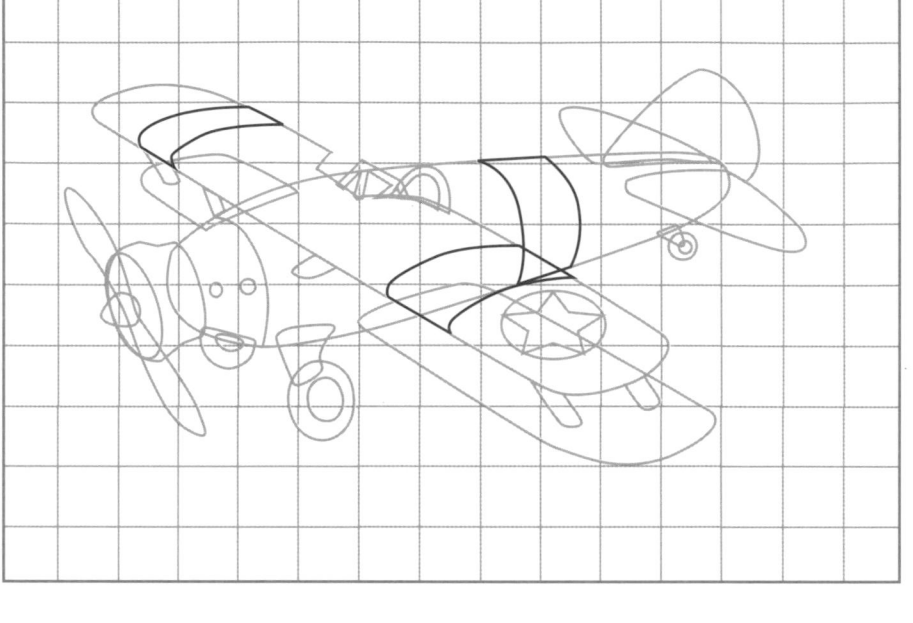

5. Draw wide stripes on the upper wings and midway on the body.

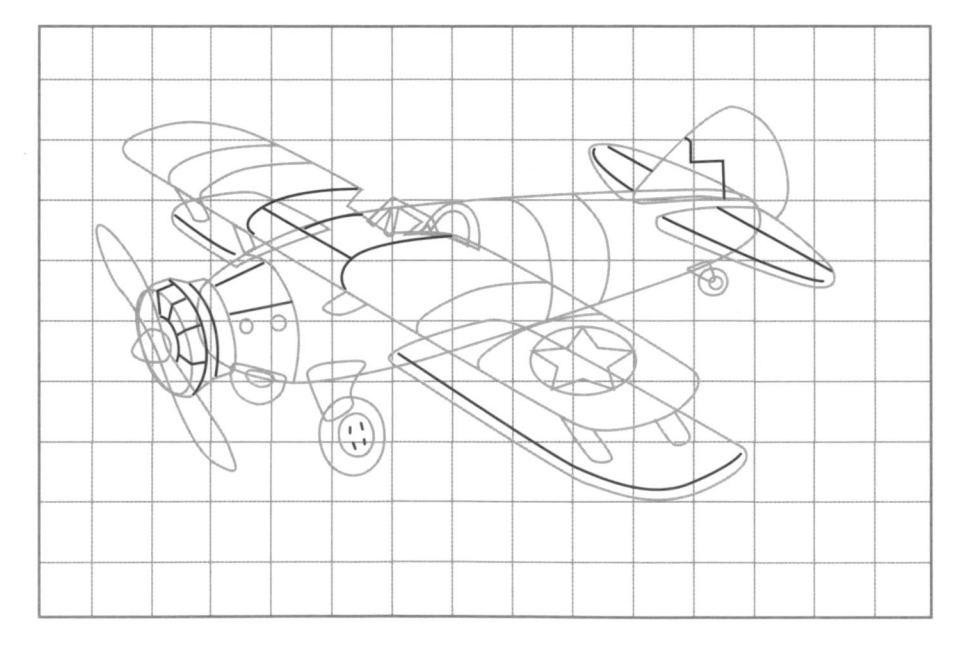

6. Add detail lines on the front wheel, nose, wings, and tail.

20

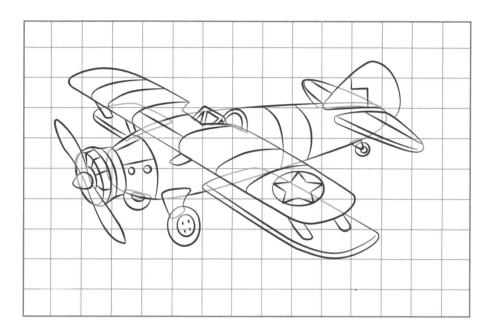

7. Use a felt-tip pen to trace the lines you want to keep.
Erase the extra pencil lines.

A permanent felt-tip pen is useful for tracing if you want to use watercolor paints for coloring.

Space Shuttle

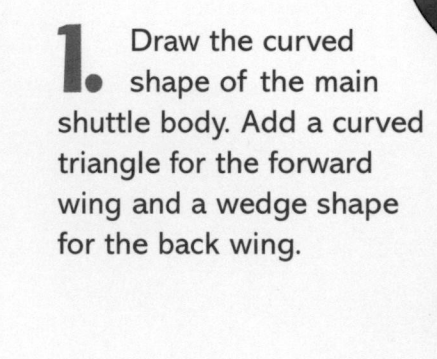

1. Draw the curved shape of the main shuttle body. Add a curved triangle for the forward wing and a wedge shape for the back wing.

2. Draw a tall wedge shape at the back of the shuttle for the tail fin. Add rectangles on both wings and the tail fin. Outline the closest wing and the closest tip of the nose to add depth. Add a rounded nose cone.

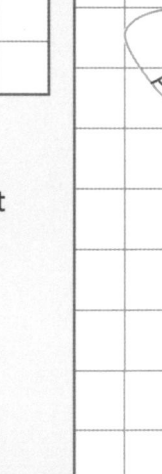

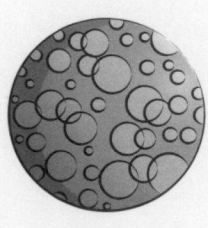
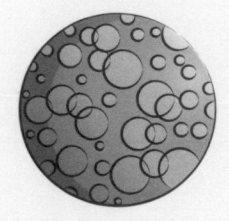

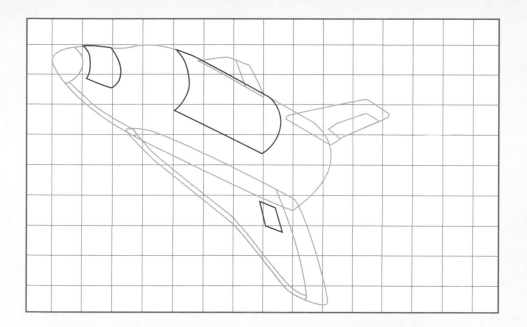

Don't be afraid to try new sketches. You can always erase and redraw.

3. Draw two curved rectangles to create the cargo bay doors and a hatch on the nose of the shuttle. Add a rectangle for a hatch detail on the closest wing.

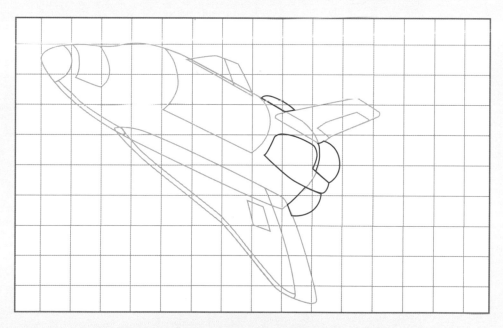

4. Sketch four rounded shapes toward the back of the shuttle for the engine pods.

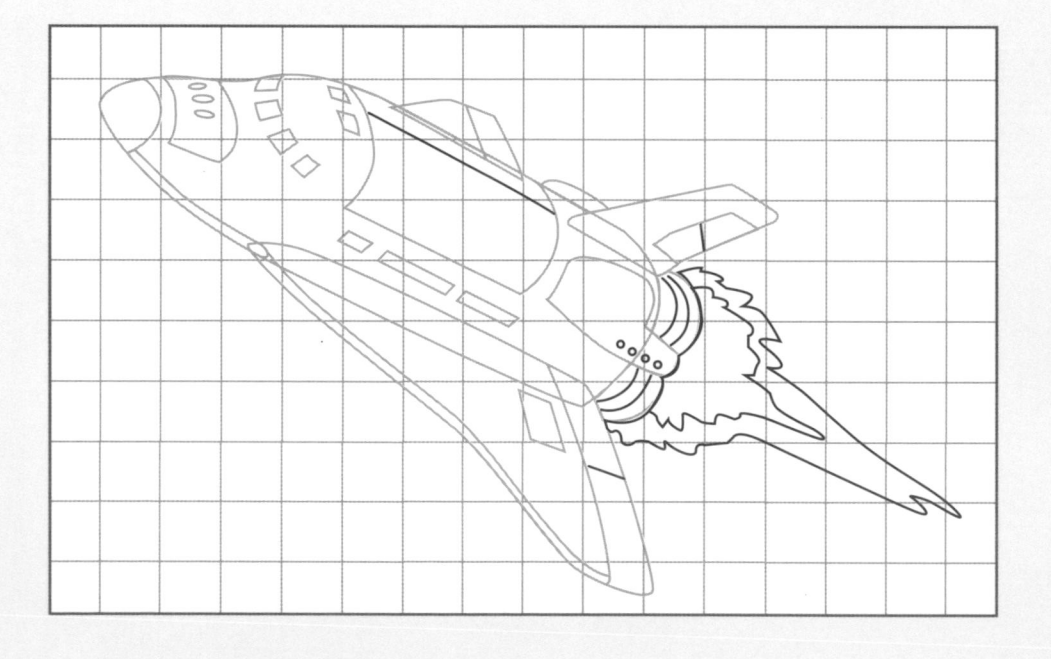

5. Draw rectangles for the cockpit windows as well as hatch details on the body. Add three narrow ovals to the hatch on the nose.

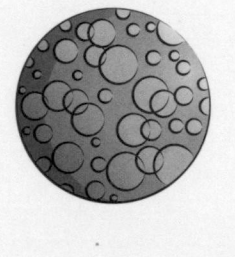

6. Draw line details on the wings, bay door, and fin. Sketch curved lines just beyond the shuttle for the engines. Add some small circles on the engine pod. Draw wavy lines for fire coming out of the engines.

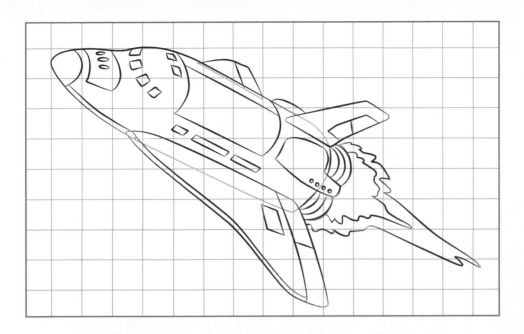

7. Trace the lines you want to keep with a felt-tip pen. Erase any extra pencil lines.

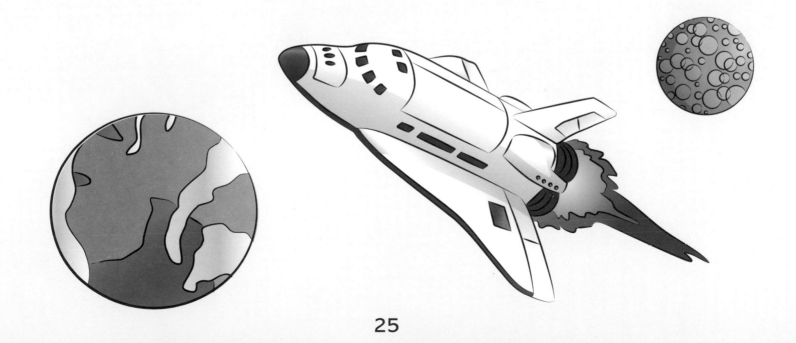

World War II Plane

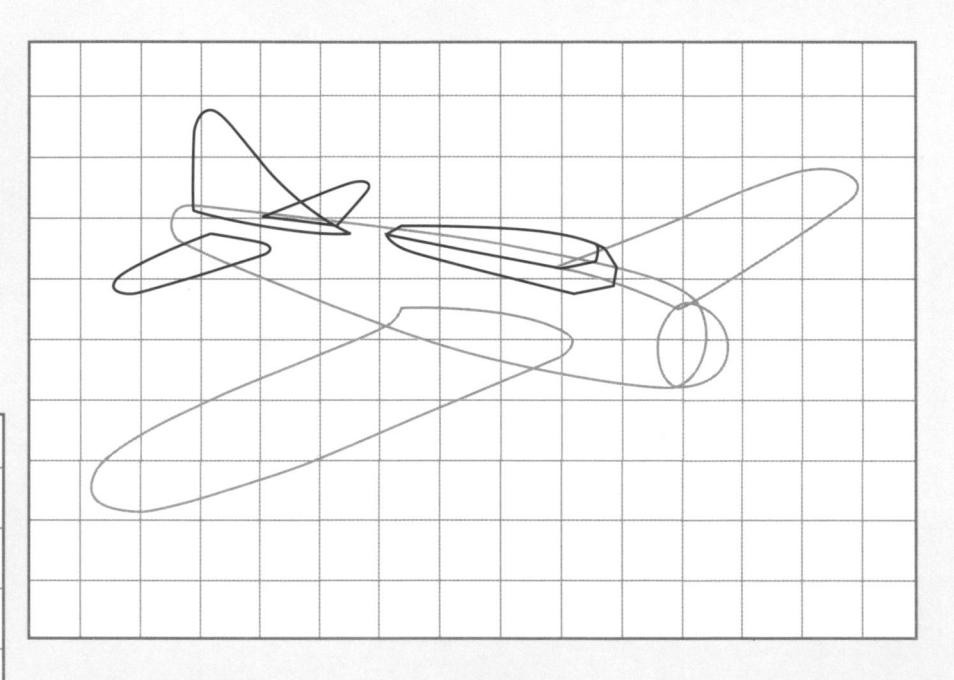

2. Draw three rounded triangles for the tail. Add a long wedge shape on top of the body for the cockpit.

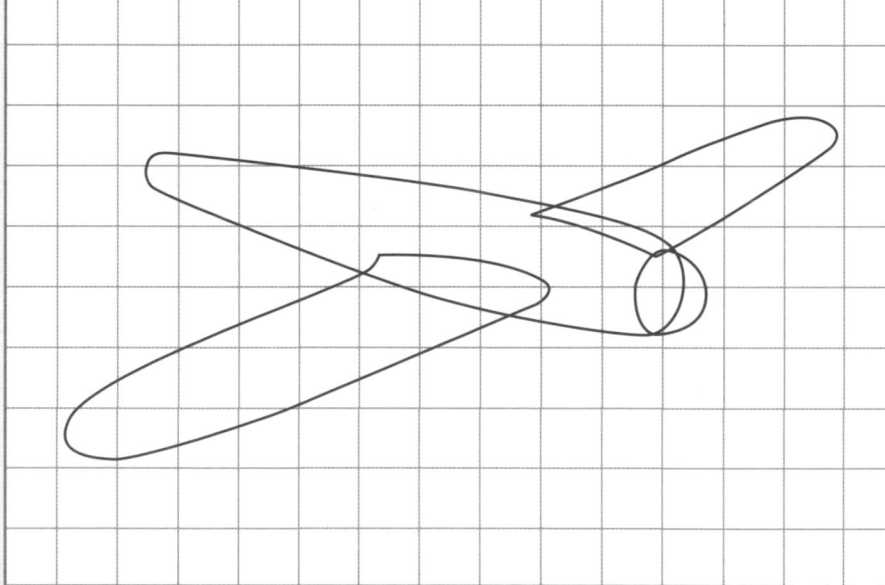

1. Draw a long oval for the body of the plane. Add an oval at the front to make the forward bubble window. Sketch the two long wing shapes.

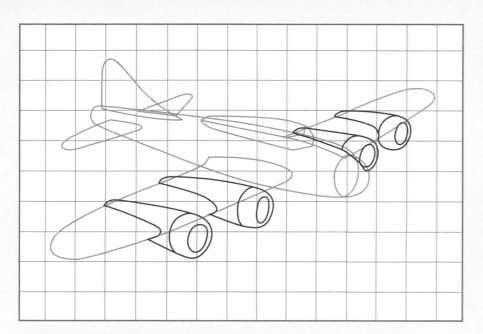

3. Sketch two cylinders on each wing to make the engines. Add a circle at the front of each cylinder. Draw a curved line behind each circle to add detail.

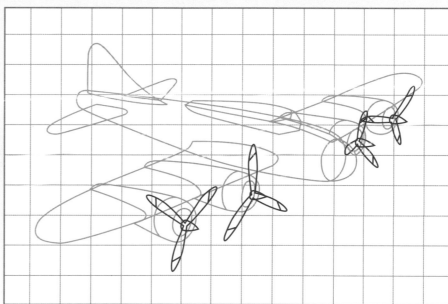

4. Draw a cone in the center of each engine circle, and add three long, thin ovals coming from each cone to form the propellers. Add a slanted detail line to the tip of each propeller.

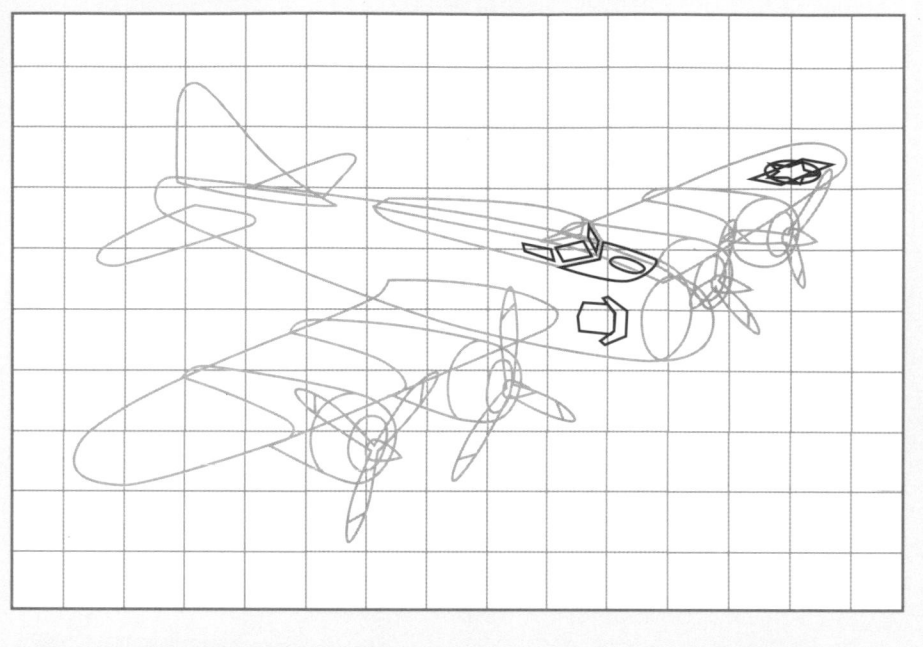

5. Draw windows on the cockpit. Sketch body details in front of the windows. Finish with a long rectangle, circle, and star emblem on the far wing.

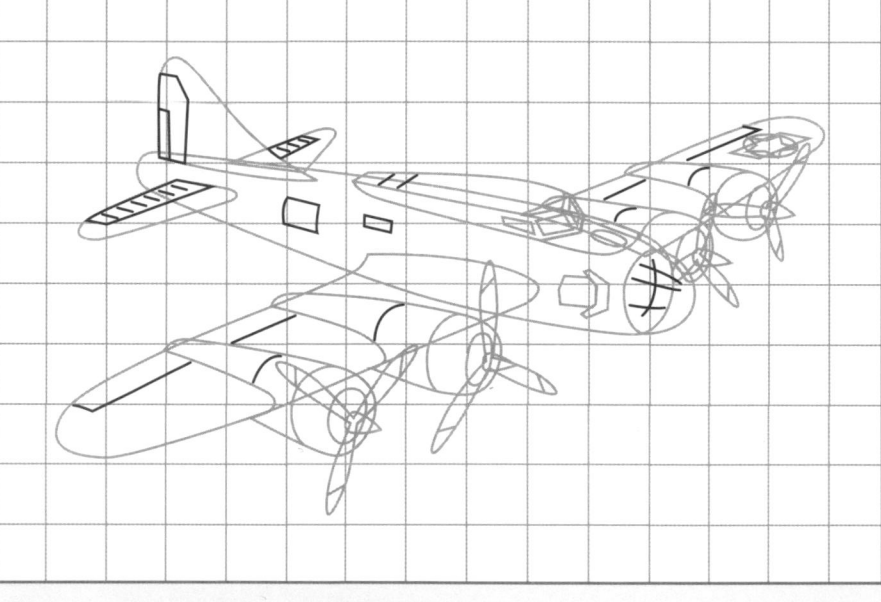

6. Add rectangles to the bottom two tail sections. Fill the rectangles in with lines. Draw a rectangle with a corner missing on the top tail section, and add a smaller rectangle inside it. Sketch line details on the wings, engines, and cockpit. Finish with a couple rectangles for hatches on the body side and some details on the front bubble window.

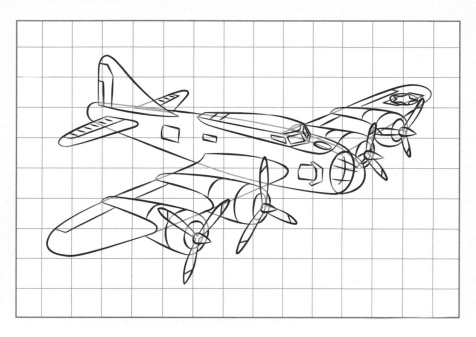

7. Trace the pencil lines you want to keep with a felt-tip pen. Erase any extra lines.

You can add more elements—such as clouds—to your drawings to make them more exciting.

Passenger Plane

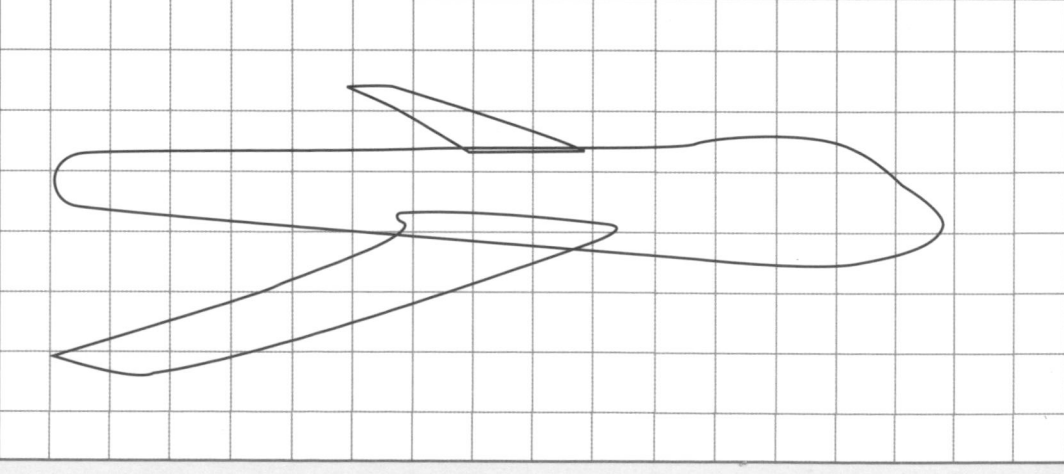

1. For the main body, draw a long, cylindrical shape with a bump at the top of one end. Add two wings coming off the body at an angle.

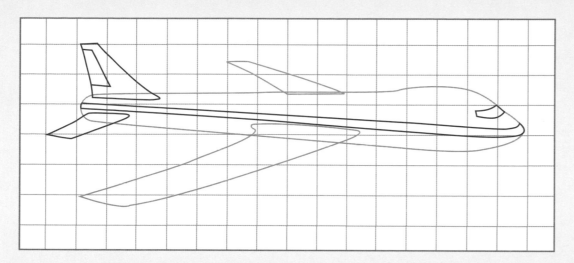

2. Draw triangular shapes for the tail section. Add a wedge shape in the top tail fin to create more detail. Draw two lines along the length of the body (curve the lines up a bit at the plane's nose). Add the curved cockpit window.

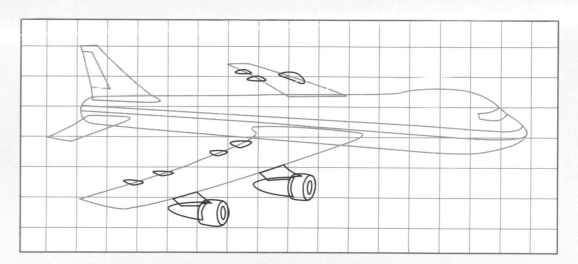

3. Draw two wedges below the nearest wing. Add bullet shapes and cylinders underneath the wedges. Draw small, rounded cones on the back side of the wing. These are the jet engines. Add two small cones and a half-circle on the far wing to indicate the engines there.

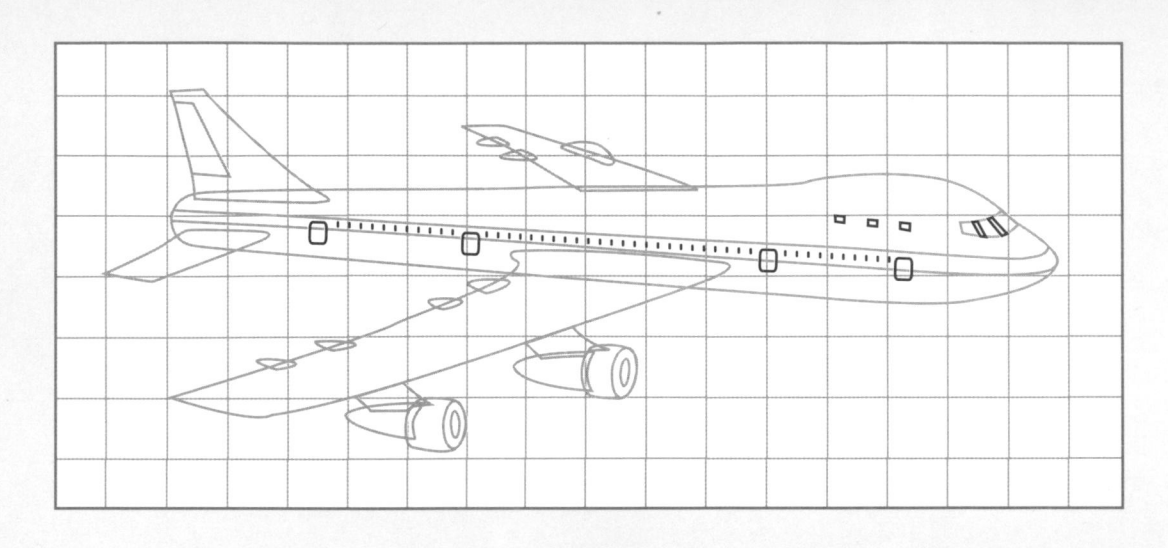

4. Draw four square-shape doors along the side of the plane. Add cockpit windows and small windows along the plane's side.

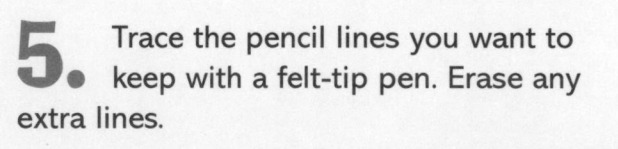

5. Trace the pencil lines you want to keep with a felt-tip pen. Erase any extra lines.

Jet

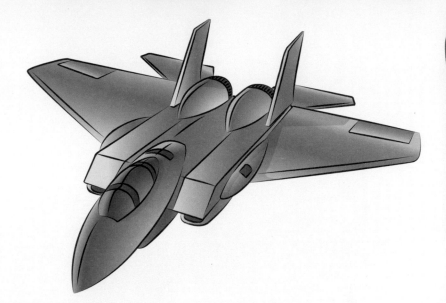

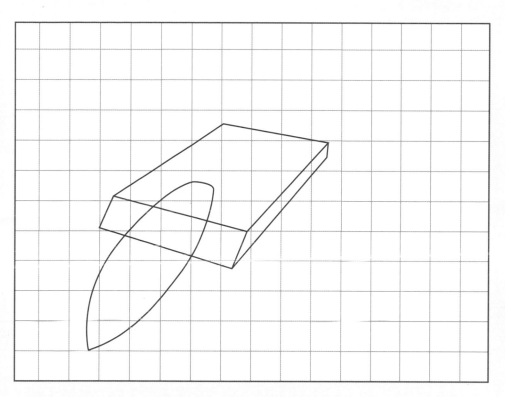

1. Draw a long, flat box form for the body of the plane. Add a long football shape for the cockpit.

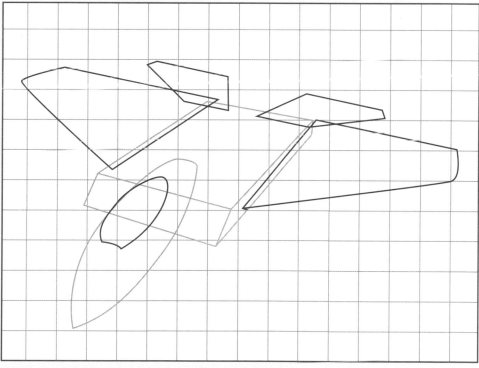

2. Sketch the window of the cockpit. Draw two large wedges and two small wedges for the wings and tail.

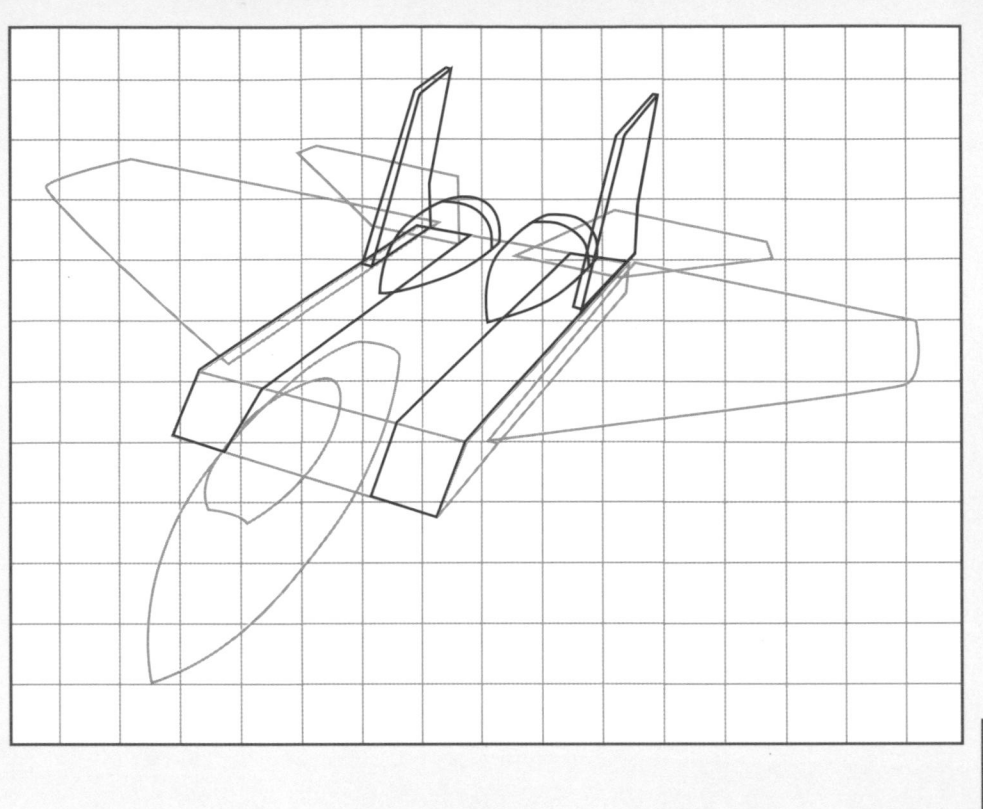

3. Draw a long rectangle on each side of the plane's body. The rectangles should stretch the entire length of the body. Add two fat bullet shapes at the back to make the engines. Sketch two curved lines for detail. Draw two tall tail fins at the back of the plane. Outline the fins to create depth.

4. Draw two long half-circles on each side of the jet body. Add an air intake on both sides of the cockpit, just under the body. Sketch narrow rectangles on the wings and a curved shape under the cockpit.

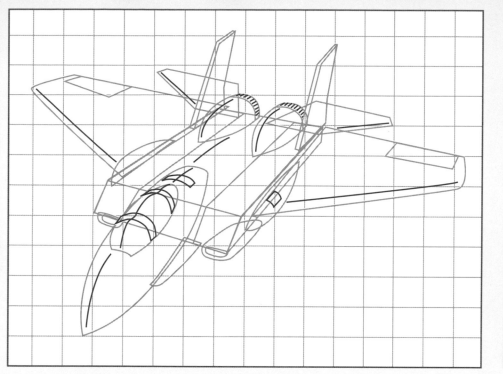

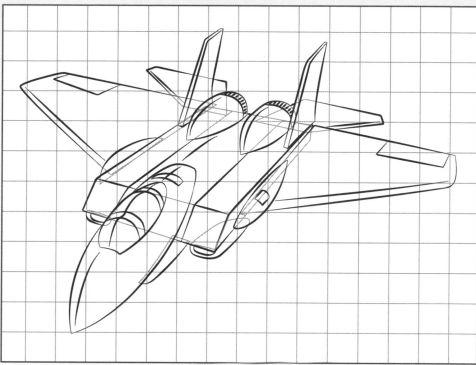

5. Draw detail lines on the wings, body, engines, and cockpit. Add some small hatches on the cockpit and on the body near the wing.

6. Use a felt-tip pen to trace the lines you want to keep. Erase any extra pencil lines.

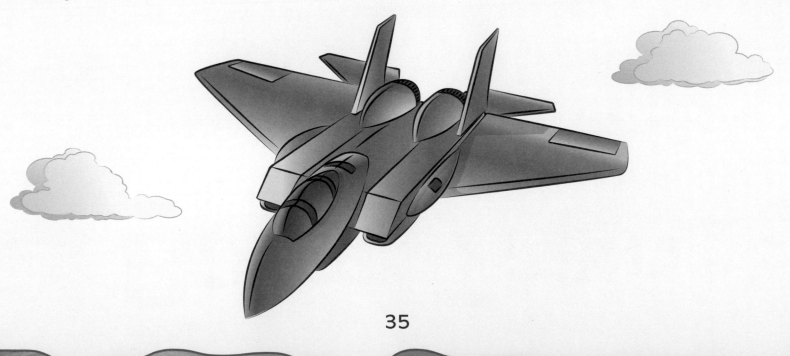

Bullet Train

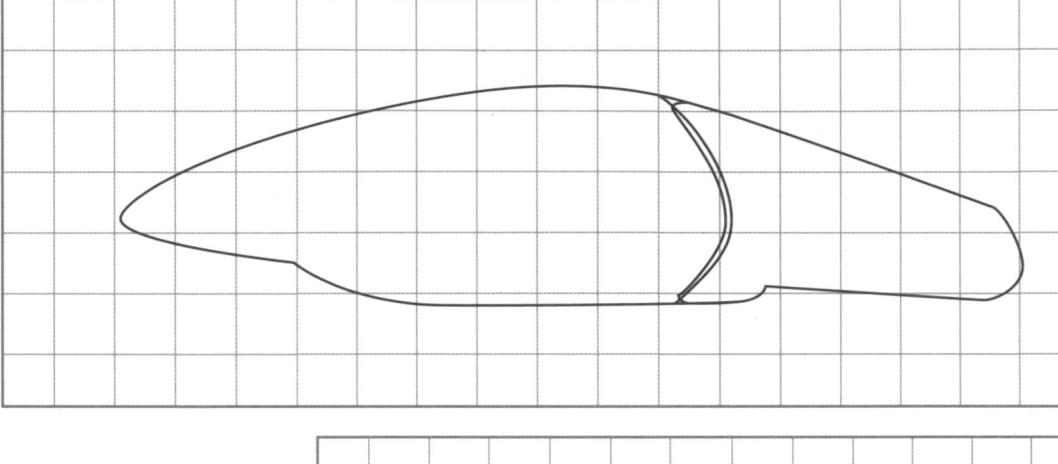

1. Draw a long, rounded shape like a banana to form the train body. Add two curved lines to divide the engine section from the passenger car.

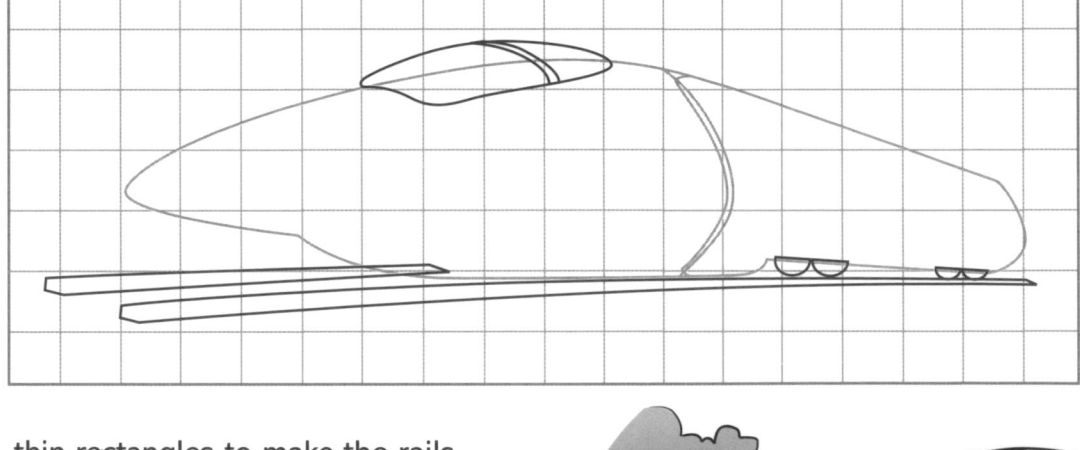

2. Draw two long, thin rectangles to make the rails (draw the longer one first and then match the perspective of the shorter rectangle to it). Sketch four half-circles at the back of the train for wheels. Add a rounded window shape at the top of the engine. Draw two curved lines to divide the window.

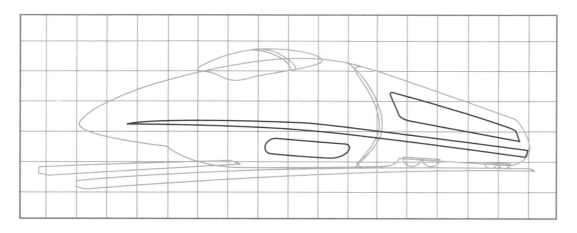

3. Draw a very skinny, long triangle across the side of the train. Add a rounded rectangle to the passenger section for a window. Sketch a long oval hatch on the bottom of the engine section.

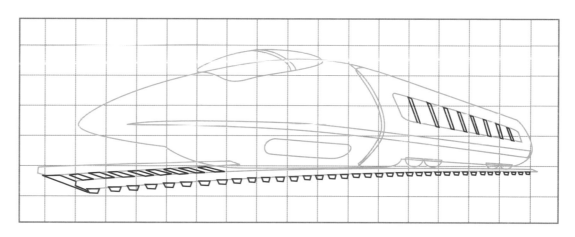

Remember that the red lines show the new steps you need to draw.

4. Draw several small, thin rectangles to divide the passenger windows. Sketch several rectangles between the rails to make the railroad ties. Finish them with small wedge shapes under the first rail.

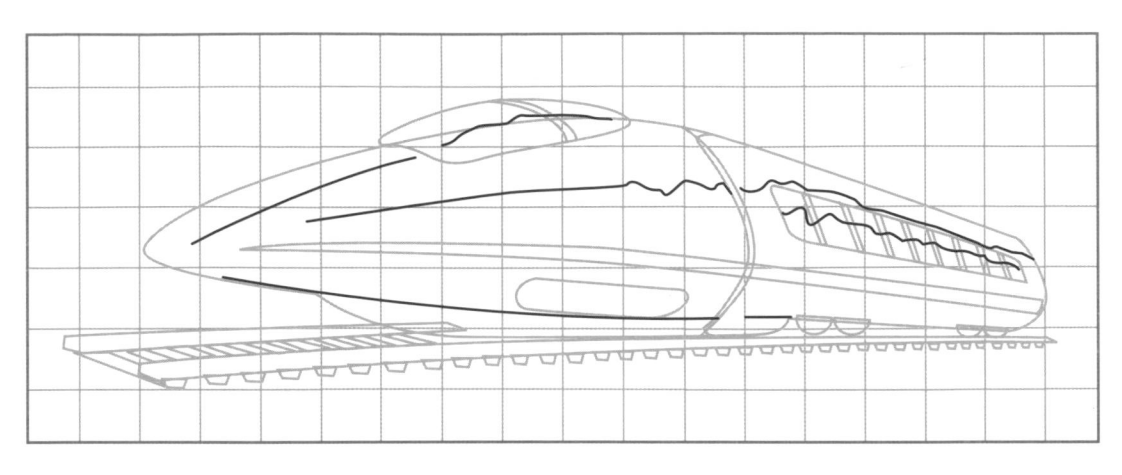

5. Draw a few curvy and straight lines following the shape of the train. These make reflections on the shiny metal surface of the train.

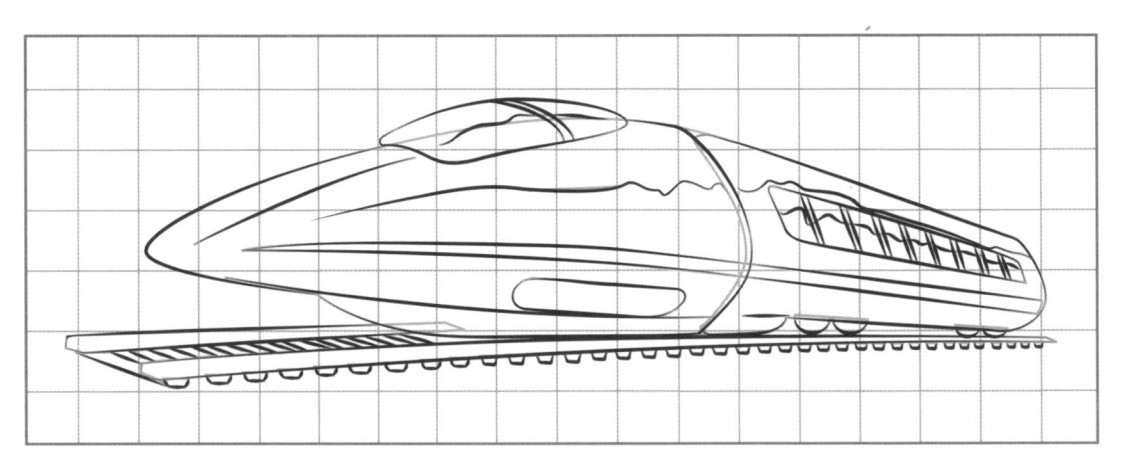

6. Trace the pencil lines you want to keep with a felt-tip pen. Erase any extra lines.

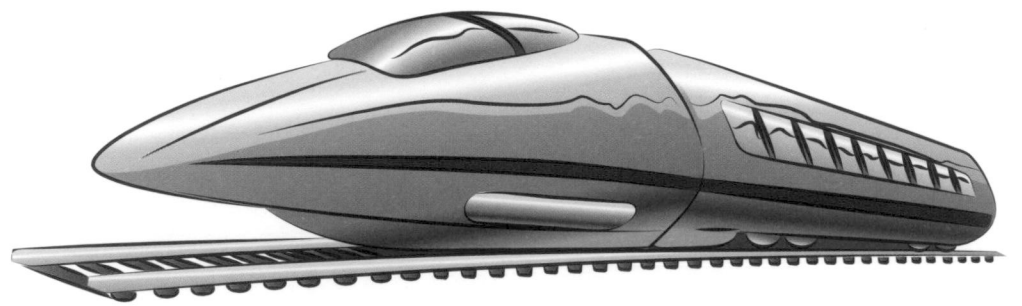

Diesel Engine

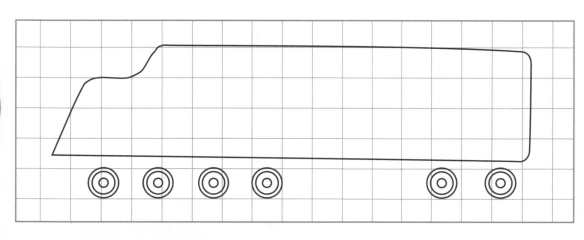

1. Draw a long, rounded train shape for the main body of the engine. Add six wheels, four toward the front and two toward the back.

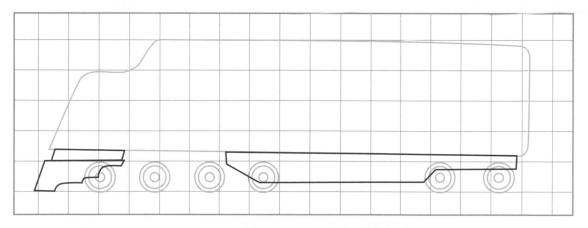

2. At the front of the car, sketch a slanted rectangle with an angled shape below it to create the wheel guard. Create the rear bottom part of the car with an angular form by the back wheels.

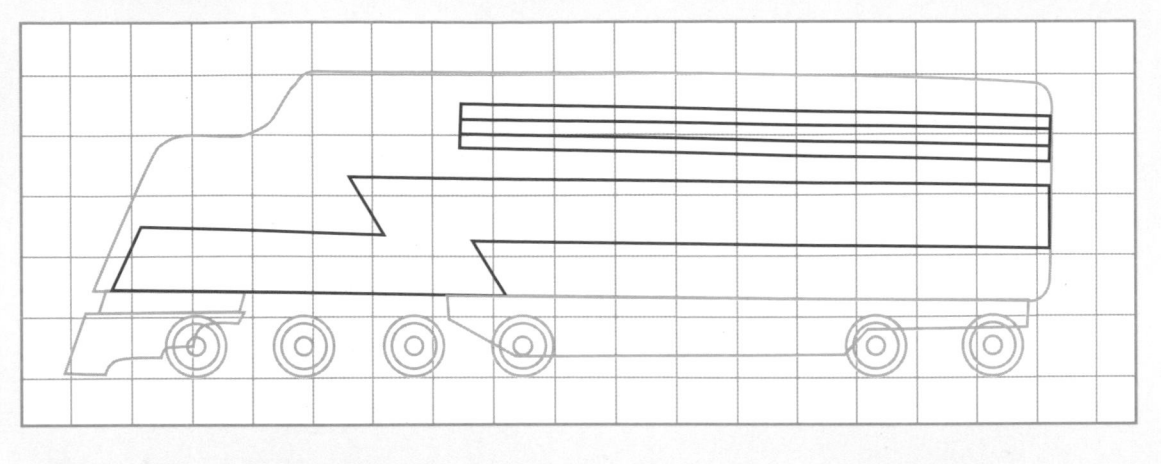

3. Draw a big, fat lightning bolt along the length of the car. Add some stacked long, thin rectangles for the windows.

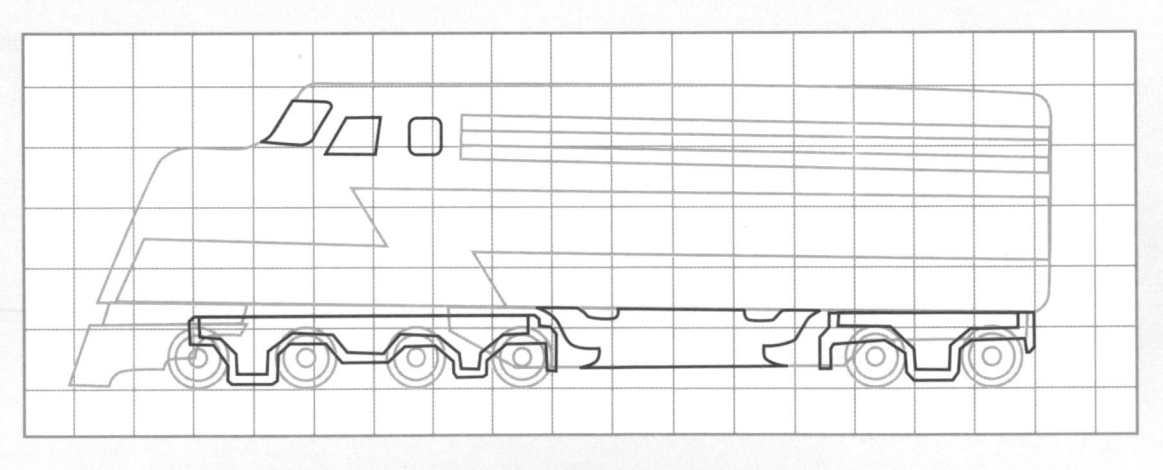

4. Draw three square shapes for the main cab windows. Add geometric shapes such as the ones shown along the lower edge of the cab. These shapes should partly cover the wheels.

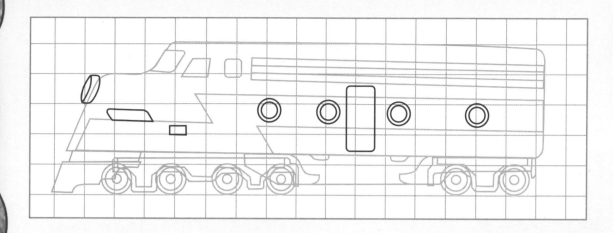

5. Draw four round windows on the side of the car. Add a door in the center and a few small rectangular hatches near the front. Sketch a flat, squat cylinder for a light on the hood.

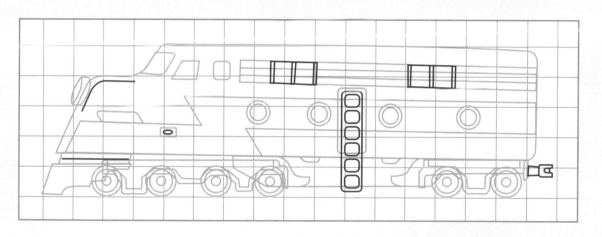

6. Use rectangles and straight vertical lines to create the two upper windows. Sketch a large ladder in the center door. Draw lines on the front of the train and a small oval in the hatch to add detail. Add a coupling hook (shaped like the end of a wrench) to the back of the engine.

7. Trace the pencil lines you want to keep with a felt-tip pen. Erase any extra lines.

Markers are good to use for bright, flat colors on your drawings.

Tanker Car

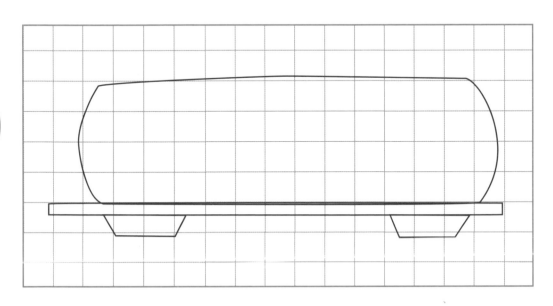

1. Draw a long, thin rectangle for the base of the tanker car. On top, add a rectangle that is curved on both ends. Sketch two wedges below the base to create the wheel supports.

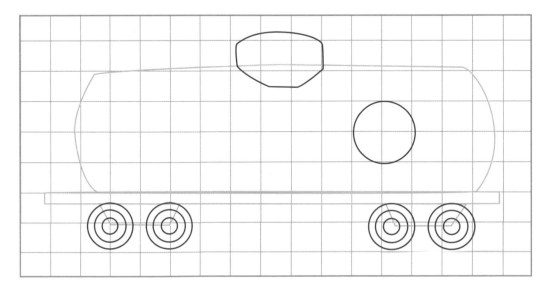

2. Draw four wheels made up of circles within circles. Add a large circle on one side of the tank. Draw a wedge shape at the top of the tank's center.

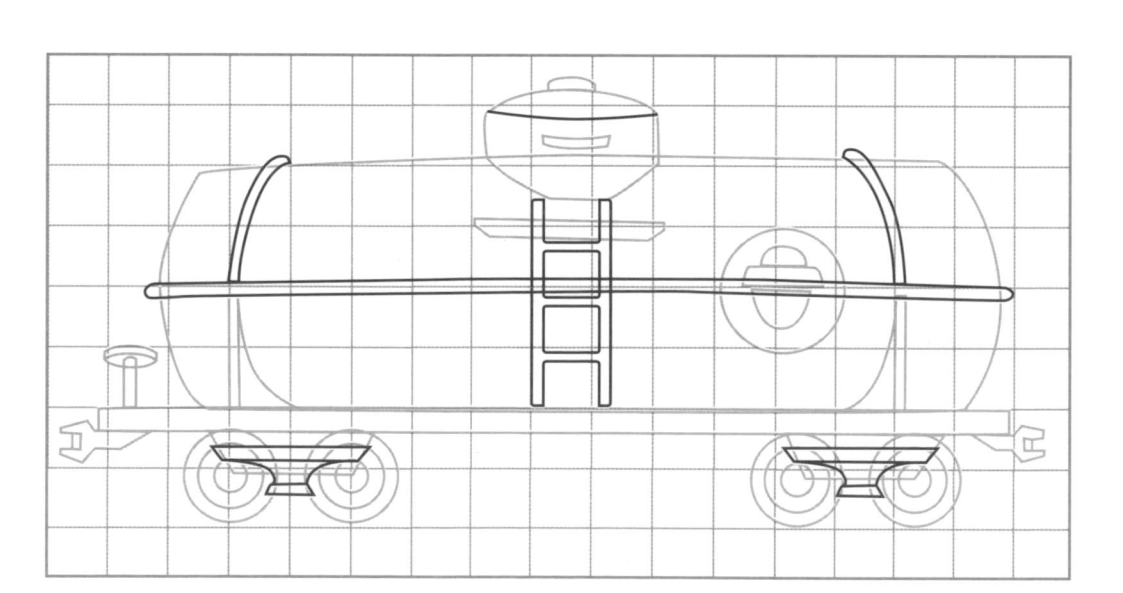

3. Sketch two half-circles and a rounded-off rectangle in the circle on the side of the car. Add rectangles for details on the tank's top and side. Draw two thin, vertical rectangles on both ends of the tank to make the supports. Finish them with an arched triangle. Draw a coupling form at each end of the car. These forms look like the end of a wrench. Add a turn wheel at the front of the car.

4. Draw a curved shape to add dimension to the top structure. Add a long, thin bar that splits the tank in two. Add two curved bars extending up from the tank supports. Sketch a ladder in the center of the car. Finish with two axle structures by the wheels.

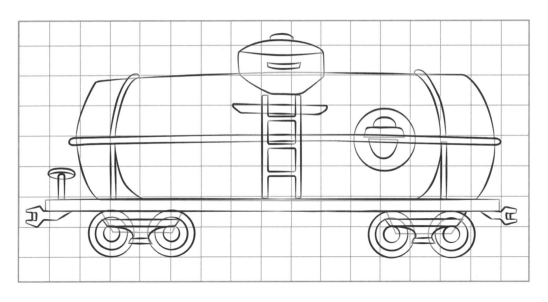

5. Trace the pencil lines you want to keep with a felt-tip pen. Erase any extra lines.

Try blending different colors together. This will help make your drawing look more realistic.

Caboose

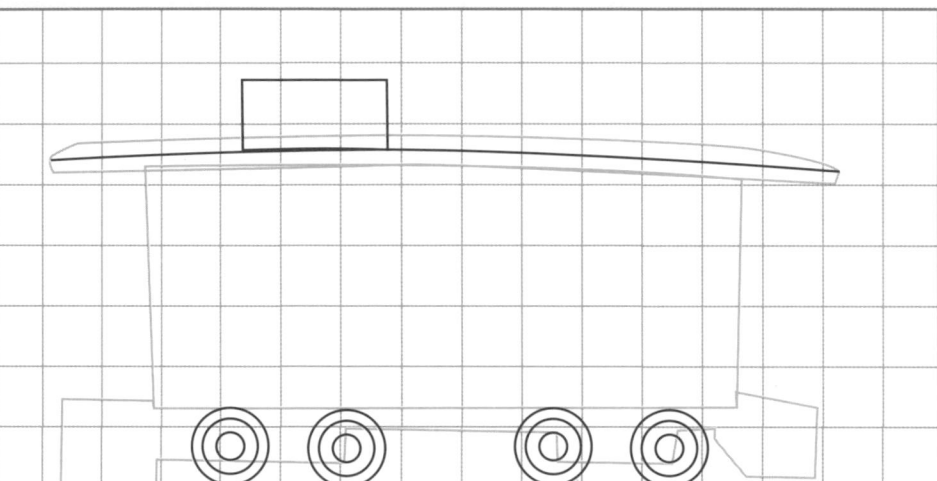

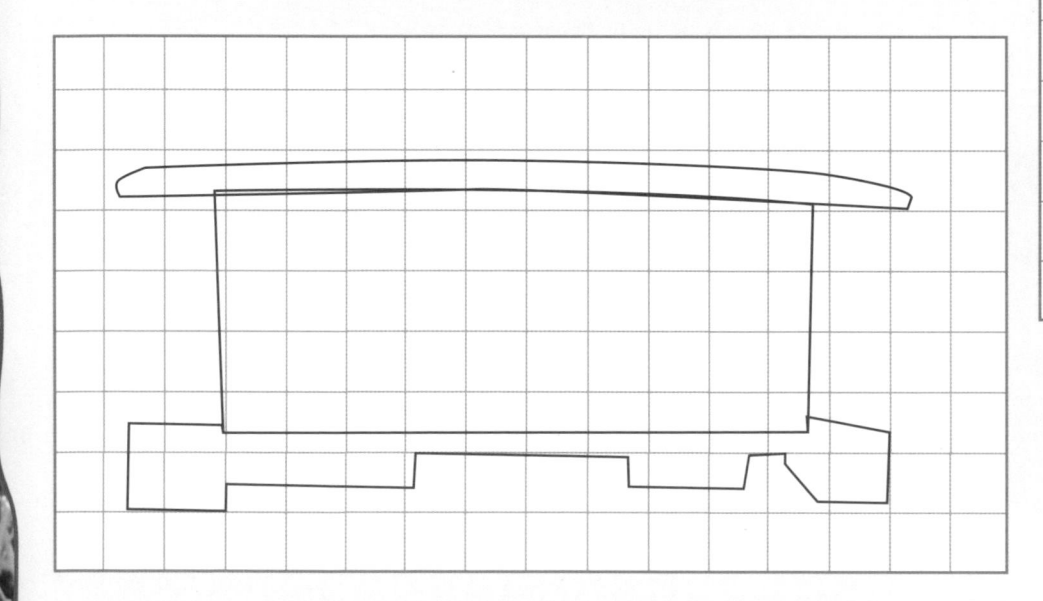

1. Draw a large rectangle for the body of the caboose. Add a long, thin, rounded-off rectangle on the top (it should be longer than the big rectangle). Sketch a shape with lots of angles to become the bottom of the car (make sure it extends past the first rectangle).

2. Draw four wheels made up of circles within circles. Sketch a long line to add depth to the roof, and draw a small rectangle on top of the roof.

46

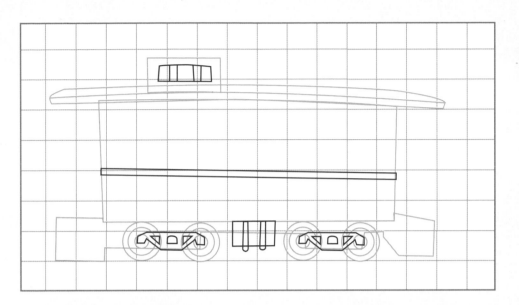

3. Draw a long, skinny bar across the car's side. Connect the wheels with an axle structure as shown, and draw two triangles and a rounded rectangle in each axle to add detail. Add windows to the small upper rectangle. Sketch a rectangle between the sets of wheels, and add two vertical rectangles with rounded ends for detail.

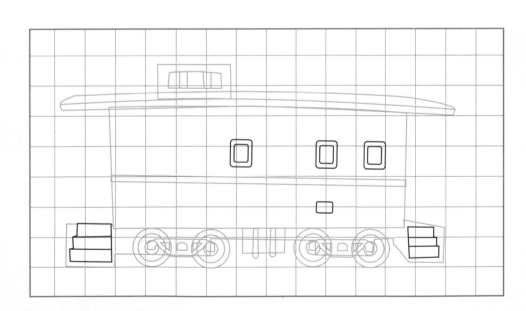

4. Draw three windows on the side of the caboose. Add a small rectangular hatch on the car's lower side. Draw three stacked rectangles for steps on both ends of the caboose (start with the bottom step, and make each new rectangle a little shorter than the last one).

47

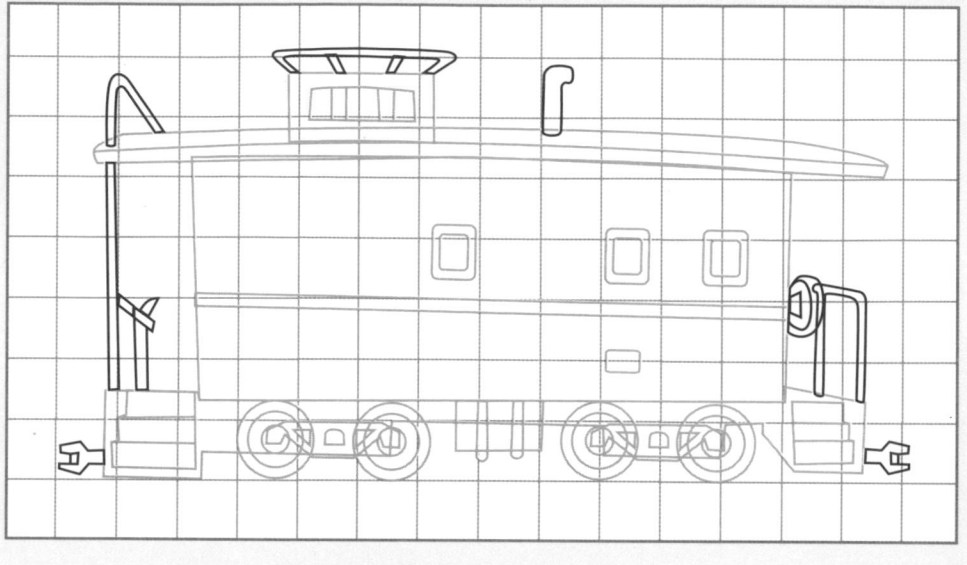

5. Draw railings on both ends and on top of the small roof box. Add a pipe coming out of the roof's center and two half-circles and a wedge shape at the back to create a turnwheel. Add a shape like the end of a wrench to both ends of the caboose.

6. Use a felt-tip pen to trace the lines you want to keep. Erase any extra pencil lines.

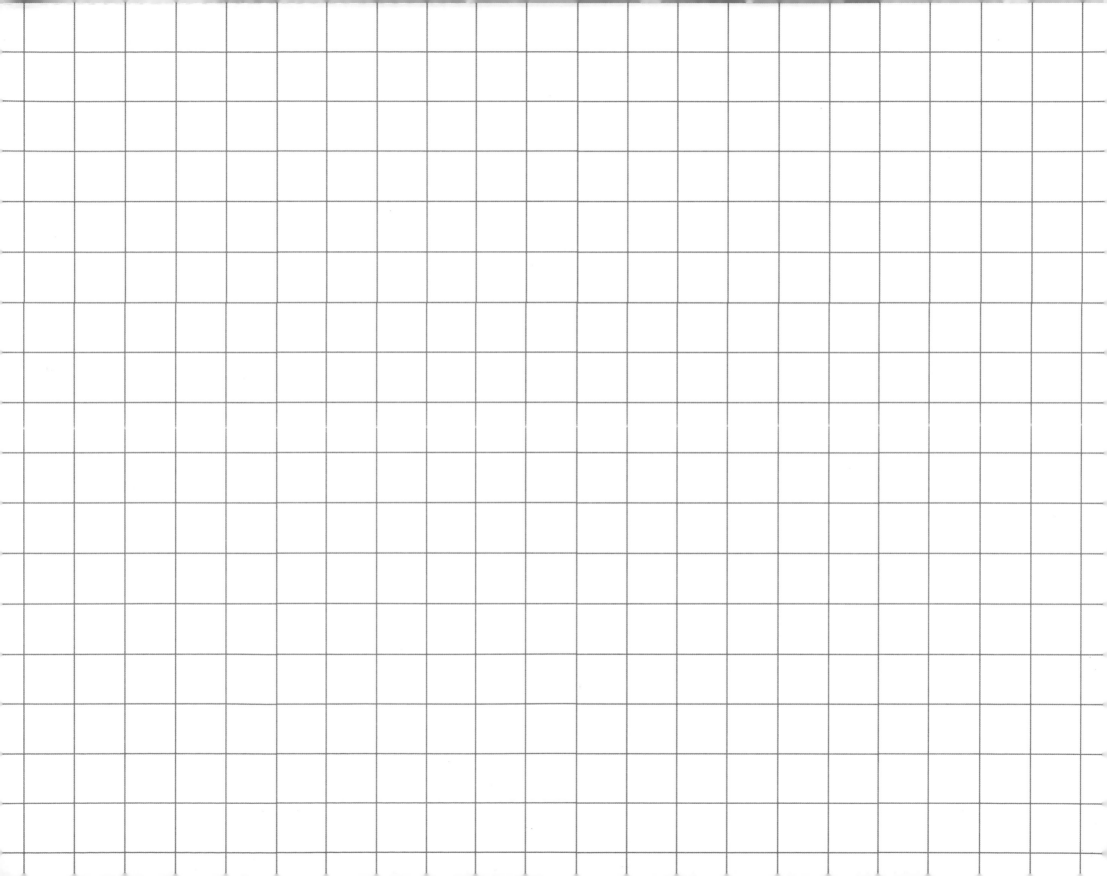

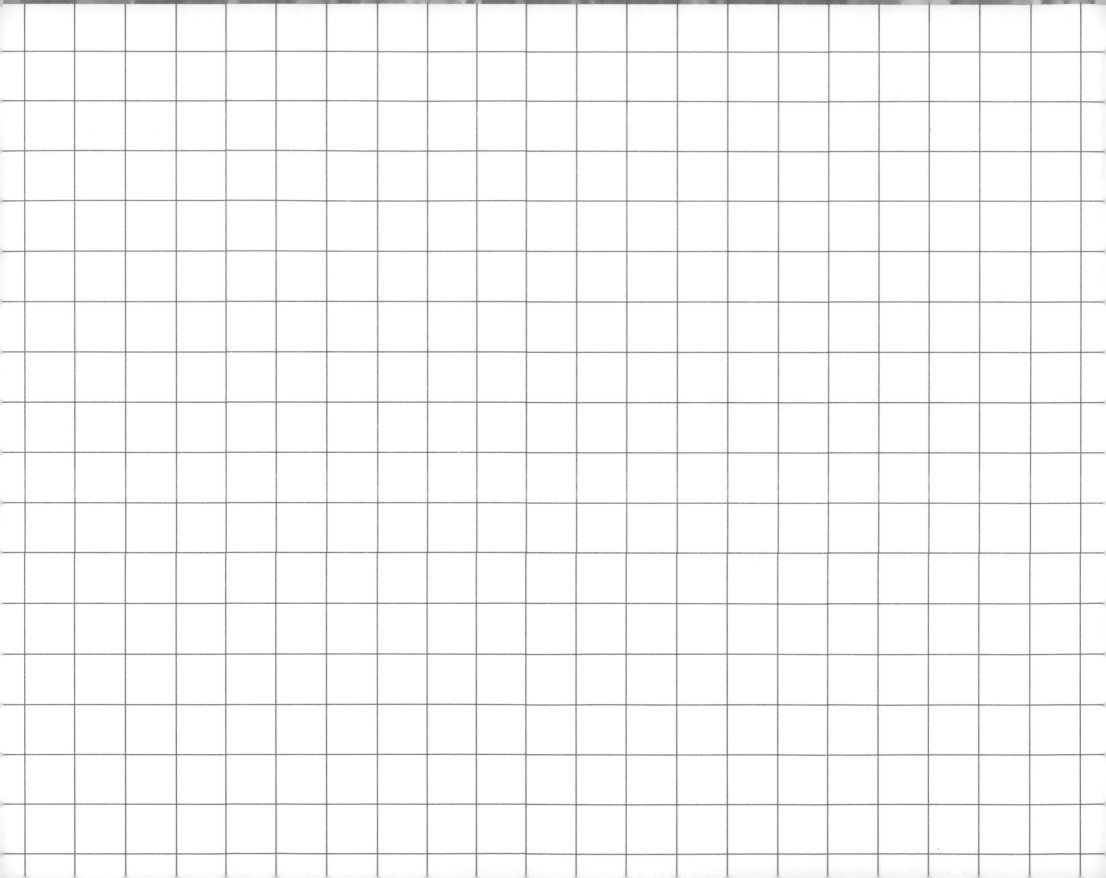

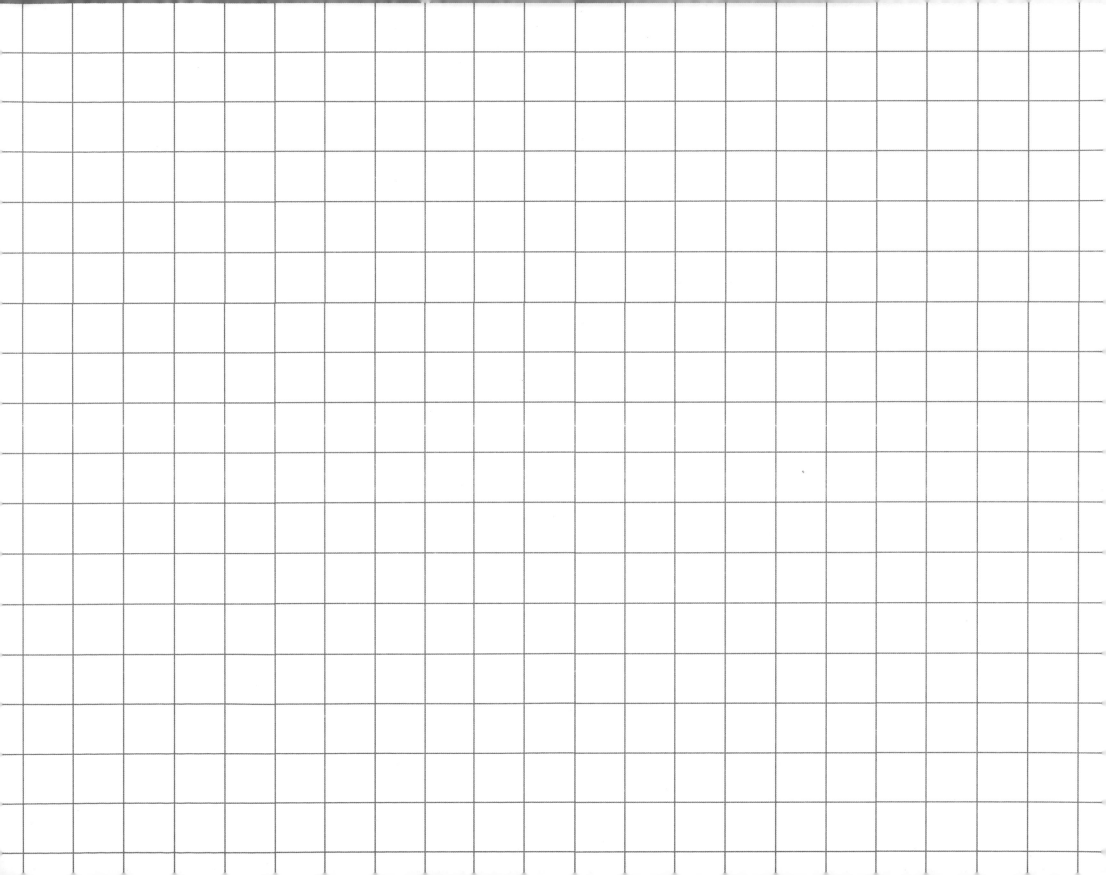

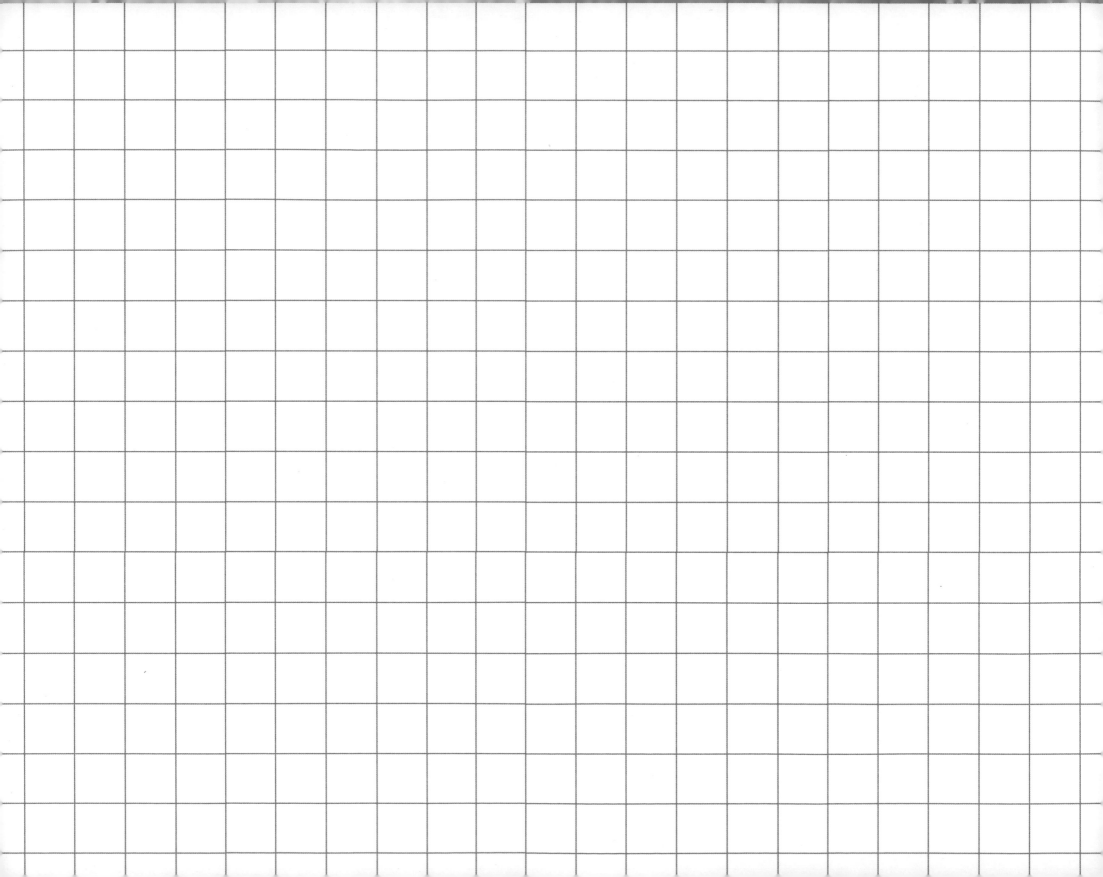

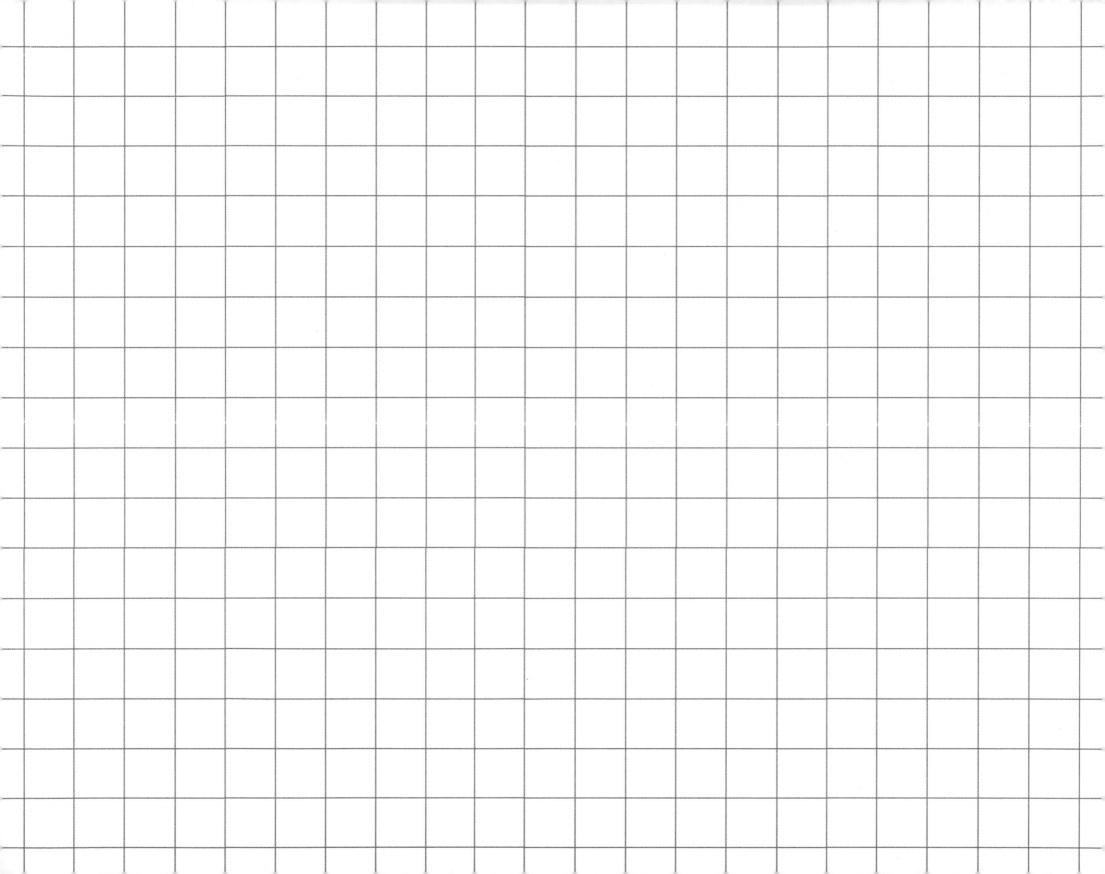

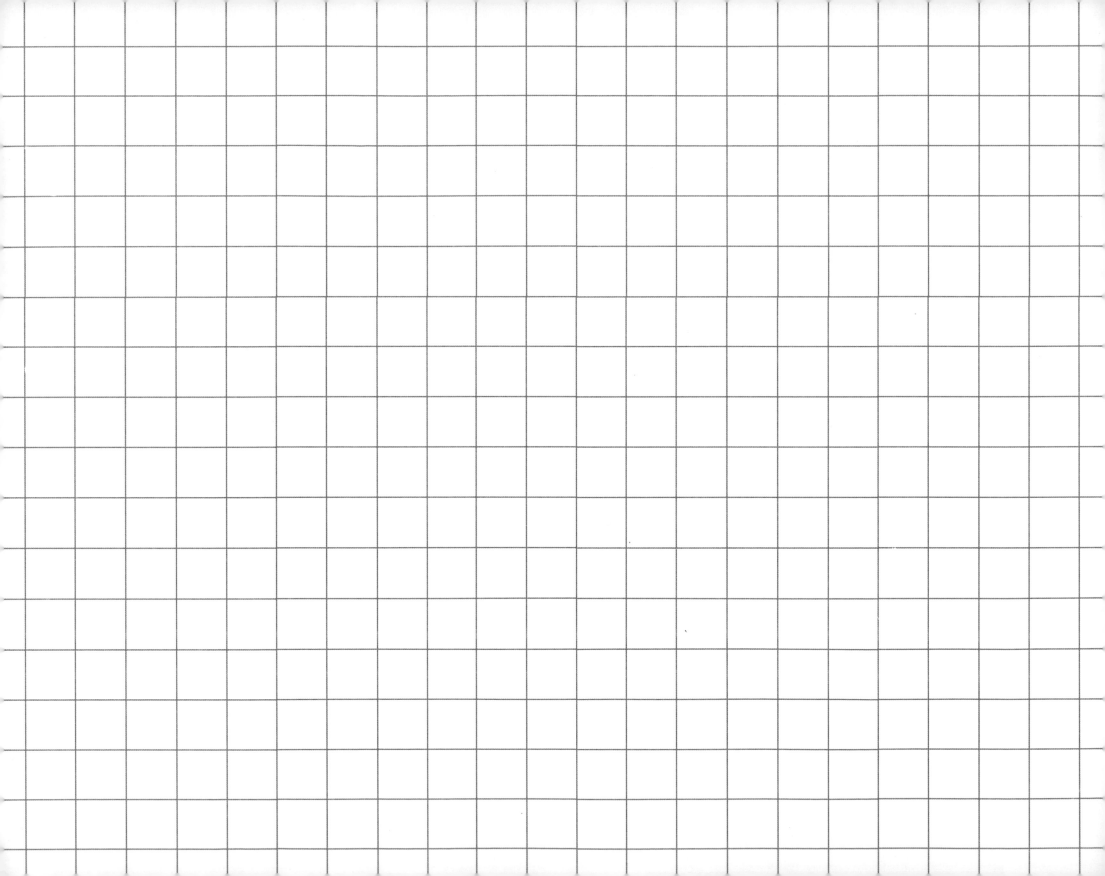